Spiritual Maturity in the Later Years

Spiritual Maturity in the Later Years

James J. Seeber, PhD
Editor

The Haworth Press
New York • London

Spiritual Maturity in the Later Years has also been published as the *Journal of Religious Gerontology*, Volume 7, Numbers 1/2 1990.

The Haworth Press, Inc., 10 Alice Street, Binghamton, NY 13904-1580
EUROSPAN/Haworth, 3 Henrietta Street, London WC2E 8LU England

Library of Congress Cataloging-in-Publication Data

Spiritual maturity in the later years / James J. Seeber, editor.
    p. cm.
    Proceedings of a conference called "Spiritual Maturity and Wholeness in the Later Years: Theory Building for Empirical Practice" held April 23-25, 1987 in Claremont, California.
    Published also as v. 7, no. 1/2 (1990) of the Journal of religious gerontology.
    Includes bibliographical references.
    ISBN 1-56024-050-4 (alk. paper). — ISBN 1-56024-051-2 (pbk. : alk. paper)
    1. Aged — Religious life — Congresses. 2. Emotional maturity — Religious aspects — Congresses. I. Seeber, James J.
BL625.4.S66 1990
248.8'5 — dc20
                                 90-43127
                                 CIP

Spiritual Maturity
in the Later Years

CONTENTS

ABOUT THE EDITOR

James J. Seeber, DMin, PhD, Associate Professor of Sociology and Director of the Gerontology Progam at California Baptist College in Riverside California, has been involved in the fields of religion and social services for over 20 years. Dr. Seeber has served 25 church congregations as either their regular or interim pastor as he has continued his education in relation to the role of ministry in the lives and well-being of older people. Dr. Seeber is on the Board of Directors of the American Society on Aging and is the Chair of the Forum on Religion and Aging. He also serves as a member of the Religion and Aging Committee of the Association for Gerontology in Higher Education and is a member of the American Sociological Association, the National Interfaith Coalition on Aging, the Society for the Scientific Study of Religion, and The Gerontological Society of America. Currently, Dr. Seeber is a geriatric consultant and continues his religious ministry as a chaplain in a local retirement home.

EDITORIAL

Spiritual Maturity and Wholeness – A Concept Whose Time Has Come

Recognizing the emerging body of literature that deals with religion and aging, a conference was convened in Claremont, California on April 23-25, 1987 to deal with the conceptual interface of religion and aging. It was called "Spiritual Maturity and Wholeness in the Later Years: Theory Building for Empirical Practice."* The goal of the conference was to define spiritual maturity and relate it to systems of thought in theology, medicine and psychotherapy. One step toward wholeness in living is seeking to integrate conceptually major fields which affect our lives. The conference was planned to help academics and practitioners share with and hear one

*The conference was sponsored by the Institute for Religion and Wholeness, School of Theology at Claremont. Co-sponsors included the American Society on Aging, American Association for Retired Persons, Fuller Theology Seminary, and Theological Student Fellowship of the Intervarsity Christian Fellowship.

1

another. A total of 24 papers were presented over a 2-1/2 day period.

Four outstanding scholars led the conference forward. David Moberg, sociologist at Marquette University and godfather of the religion and aging research field was the opening keynoter. His paper, "Spiritual Maturity and Wholeness in the Later Years" was comprehensive and provocative. Barbara Pittard Payne, Director of the Georgia State University Gerontology Center spoke on "Spiritual Maturity and Meaning-Filled Relationships." She began a process long overdue of relating spiritual change to the social processes perhaps best described by symbolic-interactionist theory in sociology. Jim Birren, psychologist at the University of Southern California Andrus Gerontology Center considered "Spiritual Maturity in Psychological Development." In addition, Bill Clements from the School of Theology at Claremont and editor of the *Journal of Religious Gerontology* presented "Spiritual Development in the Fourth Quarter of Life." The four keynote addresses are included in this volume. Interspersed among these four sessions at the conference were twenty theory-presenting papers of which twelve are included in this and an upcoming issue of *JRG*. Conceptual papers varied in content from the search for meaning (Kimble) to humor as a psychological sign of spiritual maturity (McFadden) to a theology for serving the oldest-old (Ellor). Practice or research-based topics ranged across issues from liturgical celebrations for the later years (Robb) to a report on faith development (Stokes) to ministry with Alzheimer's patients.

Several features of this historic conference stand out. One is the fully ecumenical and interfaith nature of the search for understanding in religion and aging. Numerous denominations and no-denominations were represented among the presenters and conference participants. An issue yet to be addressed among the religious traditions is that of particularism in attitude and practice compared to universalism and interfaith generalizability. It was recognized by Moberg but not faced in the conference. A second feature was the interdisciplinary nature of the religion and aging movement. Certainly there are many formally trained religion professionals. There are also many others in the helping professions with a wholeness orientation who utilize religious resources in their lives and work.

A third concern arising from the conference is the desperately growing need for research at both conceptual and empirical levels. Religion and aging research is complicated in that the psychology and sociology of religion fields are multi-dimensional in nature. Measurement instruments are few and most suffer from limited reliability or validity. At the same time, gerontological instruments which measure constructs that parallel or overlap with spirituality are few and seldom have developed respected levels of reliability either.

A fourth concern is the desire to create a future in the human services field that is capable of responding to the whole person. A conceptual foundation for religion and aging is needed that at least correlates if not blends together consistent theoretic constructs from theology, from behavioral science, and (hopefully) from medicine. Lindsay Pherigo at St. Paul Seminary, Kansas City, suggested some time ago that process theology and symbolic-interactionist sociology may make compatible bed-fellows. If some steps of deliberate correlation or blending can be taken, other aspects of concept integration may be discovered. Why shouldn't gerontology lead the academic enterprise away from the ever-splintering precipice of inquiry toward a more wholistic and perhaps more rigorous anthropology and theology of life? The papers from the Claremont conference are one step in that direction.

James J. Seeber, PhD

Spiritual Maturity and Wholeness in the Later Years

David O. Moberg, PhD

SUMMARY. Nuturing spiritual wellness is a prominent goal of most religious groups and is central to wholistic health. Although spirituality is very important to most older people and spiritual well-being and maturity are relevant to gerontological theories, consensus on criteria for evaluating them is not yet complete, and mainstream gerontology tends to ignore the subject. Two paradigmatic orientations are dominant; one extrinsically seeks self-gratification; the other is intrinsic, self-denying, and self-centered. It is important to face the divergent values about this and related topics like death and dying, the afterlife, the "new ageism" in services with and for the aging, the value-denying compromises of alleged neutrality, the danger of reification, and the tendency to ignore spirituality by meeting only empirically observable human needs.

Because so much attention is given to "spiritual" matters in contemporary American life, Leech claims that we are in the midst of a "spiritual explosion" and warns that in every such period "there is serious danger that we come to believe that any spirituality is better than none."[1] That there also are other dangers will be evident as I share some of its background, associated problems, and future opportunities.

David O. Moberg is Professor of Sociology at Marquette University, Milwaukee, WI 53233.

This article is adapted from a keynote address prepared for the Conference on Spiritual Maturity and Wholeness in the Later Years, Claremont, CA, April 23-25, 1987.

PROGRESS RELATED TO SPIRITUAL WELL-BEING

The Spiritual Well-Being Section of the 1971 White House Conference on Aging is a landmark on this subject. It defined "the spiritual" as that which pertains to people's inner resources, especially their "ultimate concern, the basic value around which all other values are focused, the central philosophy of life—whether religious, anti-religious, or non-religious—which guides a person's conduct, the supernatural and nonmaterial dimensions of human nature."[2] Fourteen recommendations came from its delegates and ten more relevant to religion from special concerns sessions.[3] The dominant topic was the importance of explicit attention to spiritual needs. Spiritual well-being was seen as relevant to all areas of life, hence to every aspect of a national policy on aging.

In 1972 the National Interfaith Coalition on Aging (NICA) was organized. One of its first projects was a survey of ministries with and for the aging in the religious sector, including a question on spiritual well-being. Responses reflected such a wide range of implicit definitions that a workshop was convened to seek consensus on its meaning. The result was the one-sentence definition that subsequently has been at the center of NICA's activities: *"Spiritual well-being is the affirmation of life in a relationship with God, self, community and environment that nurtures and celebrates wholeness."* This definition has been adapted to fit diverse theologies, traditions, ethics, and linguistic patterns, providing leverage to groups concerned for ministries with and for the aging. It has helped others to realize that every concern for total wellness must include spiritual needs. Yet, despite its broad applicability, it has not yet made a significant impact upon gerontology and geriatrics as a whole.

There has been a significant outpouring of published materials related to religion and aging in recent years. Fecher's annotated bibliography lists 504 items,[4] and the tide of publications, especially for the religious market, is still rising.[5] Besides NICA's influential activities and significant periodicals like the *Journal of Religious Gerontology, NICA Inform*, and *Newsletter of the Canadian Institute of Religion and Gerontology*, every large denomination has materials to aid ministries with and for the aging. The sheer impact of large numbers of aging people in religious congregations has increased the awareness of the importance of ministries with and for the aging. Sessions on religious programs and services have been included in recent programs of several professional associations. These developments are grounds for optimism as we look to the future, but there also are many problems which, if not resolved satisfactorily, could be very detrimental to wholistic well-being of the aging and the ministries of religious agencies to serve them.

BIASES AGAINST RELIGION

Very little attention is given to religion and spirituality in gerontological and geriatric education. Most textbooks almost completely ignore the subject and treat the church as an insignificant portion of the service network.[6] Readers are given the impression that religion is irrelevant in contemporary society where science and technology introduce pressure to deny the existence of the sacred and the validity of religious experience.[7]

This neglect of religion is inconsistent with much evidence. Religious agencies, programs, and personnel are a major source of social, psychological, and spiritual support for the aging and elderly.[8] Gallup polls have shown that three-fourths of Americans past age 65 consider religion to be very important; over four-fifths claim their religious faith is the most important influence in their lives; 95 percent pray to God; 49 percent attend church or synagogue in an average week; two-thirds rate themselves in the three highest of ten categories for leading a Christian life, and 84 percent wish their religious faith was stronger.[9]

The neglect of religion and spirituality in gerontology has many causes, including the complexities of generalizing fairly about the tremendous range of religious ideologies and practices in our pluralistic society, the lack of funds for scholarly research because of policies in foundations and governmental agencies, the erroneous allegation that secularization is inevitable and will make religion obsolete, interpretations of constitutional provisions for religious liberty and separation of church and state that squeeze religion out of public agencies and services, misinterpretation of "freedom of religion" as "freedom from religion," personal biases against religion, and the relative dearth of research on religion and spirituality in the later years.[10] People who acknowledge no religious faith, atheists, and agnostics conclude that religion is unimportant and hence unworthy of theoretical and empirical attention. By not seeking evidence, they find none. When none is reported in scholarly resources, subsequent researchers lack reminders of the subject's relevance and also ignore it in a vicious cycle of neglect and discrimination. People in applied gerontology and geriatrics then lack scholarly evidence of its importance, ignore spirituality, and alienate themselves from potential allies accessible through religious networks.[11]

All of this contributes to the "bad press" religion typically gets in the mass media. When most "gatekeepers" are antithetical to religion, we can hardly expect positive reports and interpretations.[12] In addition, "news" consists of the unusual; spiritual orientations among the aging and positive effects of religious faith and practice on personal and societal well-being are typical or "normal," not newsworthy.

The "new ageism"[13] among religious leaders also may contribute to misinterpretations of the role of religion in the later years. By giving primary attention to conditions that can be corrected, they tend to make flaws and fallacies of religious agencies the focus of attention in reports, discussions, and programs related to aging. This lop-sided approach fails to accentuate the joys and benefits of old age and retirement, noting only the burdens and pains. It tends to demean the status of older people, emphasizes corrective and palliative services, and contributes to stereotypes of "old age" that are uncomplimentary at best and horribly frightful at worst. As a result, the self-images of older people are molded by socially reinforced pictures of disability, deterioration, and painful incapacitation in unpleasant environmental settings. The internalized expectation contributes to its fulfillment when people finally admit that they are "old." Even activity theory can backfire, for those who out of inability or personal interests do not fit the norm of being socially and physically active are labeled as failures.

DEFINITIONS

The diversity of definitions associated with spirituality produces difficulties for pragmatic discourse and for research. Religious groups that use NICA's definition of *spiritual well-being* (SWB) define major words used in it (affirmation, relationship, nurtures, etc.) differently. This also occurs in scholarly studies; dozens of implicit and explicit definitions of SWB are evident in one collection by twenty-seven sociologists.[14] Every measure of SWB is comprised of different indicators and in effect is a unique operational definition. The diversity enriches the bountiful multivariate concept when all focus validly upon the same basic phenomenon.[15] Yet in extreme instances what one interprets as reflecting SWB is viewed as a symptom of spiritual illness by another.

One can have spiritual wellness without *spiritual maturity*, just as an infant can be physically well when far from mature. SWB is a status; maturity is the result of a process of growth. Yet maturity cannot be attained without having SWB. Thus in traditional Protestantism and contemporary evangelicalism, one cannot have spiritual life without trusting Jesus Christ as Savior; without life, there can be no growth.

Among all domains for change in human lives, the one that provides the most opportunity for continuing growth in the later years is the spiritual. Those who are "spiritually dead" can find spiritual life through a new or renewed faith commitment. The spiritually immature can develop toward maturity. The relatively mature can continue to grow in wisdom and spiritual gifts. Such growth usually includes reviewing and recreating one's past, constructively mourning present losses, and ordering one's view of the future.[16] My own research interviews reveal that even the most mature Christians recognize that they have not attained the ideal level of perfect maturity. They are the most likely to recognize their need to continue growing toward "the whole measure of the fullness of Christ" (Ephesians 4:13). Others see them as "spiritual giants," but they expect to become fully mature only after leaving their earthly life.

Another pertinent concept is *wholeness*. The word "health" is from an Anglo-Saxon root meaning "hale" or "whole" but has been so medicalized that we often use it as if it refers only to the absence of physical and mental illness. A wholistic emphasis of necessity includes attention to spiritual needs. Unfortunately, even wholistic health centers have tended to be only "halfistic," for they have not given attention to industrial, governmental, economic, and social institutions and policies that impact the total health and wellness of people they serve.[17] Nor can their professional staff members be wholistic. Each is too limited, fragmented, and human to be "the compleat healer," yet all can work together as a team in which competencies of others complement their own.[18] It is the total person who is aging, so all professions related to him or her must be interfaced and integrated. At the core of each person is "the spiritual dimension [which] is the inclusive dimension for understanding and integrating theories and concepts of human development with techniques and programs for ministry with older adults."[19]

Spirituality, a concept obviously related to spiritual wellness and maturity, is easily misinterpreted. In many eastern religions and new religious movements and even some Christian groups it refers to a denial of reality, an attempt to gain consciousness of "the god that is in you," or some other form of philosophical idealism. Leech points to dangers in the "wholly inward forms of spirituality" which stress warmth and inner experience but neutralize the social conscience, uncritically celebrate the status quo of the world's temporal power structures in the comfort and false security of the existing social order, or make materialism a pejorative term in a flight from the world that pushes all hope into a future millennial age. "The spirituality of the kingdom of God is a spirituality which is rooted in the earth, in matter, and specifically in the Word of God becoming flesh," so "Christians . . . do not have to choose between the false polarities of an escapist pietism or a superficial activism."[20] Politics and prayer, action and contemplation, are united by a genuine spirituality.

Lane likewise identifies four aspects of spiritual life: A Christian outlook which is "a reflex, intellectual faith-vision of the world"; finding or seeking God in prayer and contemplation; finding God in activity that makes prayer a style of life in God's service, and "an experiential awareness of the presence of God" which is a special grace or gift of sensing God's operative presence in the world and in oneself.[21] "It is this rooting in a personal experience of God that empowers individuals and communities to become committed, creative forces for the transformation of society."[22] As an "ambassador for Christ" like St. Paul (2 Corinthians 5:20-21), "one of the best characteristics of a spirituality for our time is reconciliation, both individual and social."[23]

Protestant spiritual traditions also emphasize the important role of community; genuine spiritual life contravenes selfish individualism and has an impact upon the world. "Protestantism cannot be solely blamed for the individualism of American life. Indeed, it would seem to be the other way around: American individualism . . . has had a deleterious effect on Protestant spirituality."[24] Christian spirituality is fully consistent with, if not a central component of, spiritual maturity and wholeness. The same is true of Jewish spirituality.[25]

GERONTOLOGICAL THEORIES

Linkages of spiritual wholeness with the theoretical paradigms of gerontology can easily be established. Progressive *disengagement* from social roles is evident in many religious contexts, sometimes as a concomitant of physical deterioration but all too often also as a result of ageist policies and practices. Yet even those who no longer can attend congregational gatherings need not be fully disengaged. They can continue to be socially and spiritually involved, especially if active steps are taken to incorporate them into the spiritual life of the community.[26] Absence from religious meetings need not mean severed relationships.[27]

The ideology of *activity theory* has dominated the orientations of most religious leaders concerned with aging. Much of the denominational literature and educational materials to aid aging ministries has the goal of keeping older members actively involved in congregational and community life. Spiritual ministries of prayer, counsel, encouragement to visitors and friends, and the listening ear are significant contributions that even shut-in elderly can make,[28] and services the young-old can contribute are almost unlimited. Nevertheless, activity theory contributes to the "new ageism" when activism is presented as the only suitable way for the aging function.

Insisting that everyone must be active can be a form of tyranny, trying to force all into the same mold instead of allowing them indulge preferences for "merely" watching television, reading, praying, meditating, or other "passive" behavior. Such policies fail to recognize individual differences, view "nonactive" conduct as a symptom of maladjustment, obstruct some of the ways to nurture spiritual growth (even when opening others), and induce feelings of disappointment and failure.[29] Whenever one judges successful aging only by the retention of activities appropriate to young and middle-aged people, activity theory becomes "little more than a subtle way of glorifying youth at the expense of old age."[30]

Stage theories that presume people go through a hierarchical series of periods in the life cycle are helpful in understanding typical aging.[31] In practitioners' minds, however, they can become oppressive by implying that everyone must fit the pattern and that those who do not are mentally or spiritually ill, deficient, or inadequate. Heuristic developmental schemes must be seen as inventive creations of researchers or scholars to summarize complex sets of data, not reified into rigid prescriptive norms to control people's lives. (To do so is a form of idolatry replacing God's dominion with control by whoever is "in charge.")

Many older people think in terms of *exchange theory*, feeling that they must compensate tangibly for every service and favor received by equivalent gifts or pay. Usually they fail to recognize important non-material gifts of cheer, counsel, prayer, thankfulness, and simple listening to others. These are spiritual services which older people can provide par excellence, but which usually are ignored in the menus of services suggested for interpersonal and intergenerational exchanges. The life review process of telling one's life story also can greatly benefit listeners or readers as well as the narrators.[32]

The *person-environment transaction* perspective, which emphasizes the interaction and mutual influence of the individual and environment, underscoring the potential for growth and development throughout the entire lifespan,[33] and other theories of aging also are important.

All theories are tools, not ends. Each has limitations, as well as strengths and virtues. An important unfinished task in gerontology is to analyze the reciprocal and interactive implications of spiritual wellness and maturity in each theory, as well as the ways in which the theories all complement, modify, and correct each other. Biological theories of aging tend to be "tautological or empty formulations, tending merely to restate observations, or else [to] insist on a partisan, unproved view."[34] Most social and behavioral theories are similarly deficient, merely describing central tendencies. *The inclusion of theoretical and empirical contributions on the spiritual nature, needs, and resources of humanity can become one of the most important developments in social gerontology.* Any attempt to develop complete understanding of aging without attention to the human spirit is rightly labeled "holistic" instead of "wholistic," for a huge hole replaces its core!

CRITERIA TO EVALUATE SPIRITUAL GROWTH

Basic to professional and scholarly work in this domain is the question of how to determine whether people are or are not spiritually well and growing toward spiritual maturity. Religious literature is richly endowed with philosophical and theological interpretations and recommendations, but most of the criteria are vague, focus upon attitudes, beliefs, and feelings that are not directly observable, and are linked with ideologies unacceptable to adherents of other interpretations.

Concepts of what constitutes spiritual wellness, wholeness, and "wholistic religion" are the foundation for research tools and diagnostic instruments. A central core of indicators (items like attitudinal statements or specific behaviors) may characterize SWB by virtue of our common humanity, providing a basis for generalized measures, while criteria unique to fundamentalists, traditional Catholics, charismatics, theological liberals, or other Christian groups, or to Orthodox Jews, Reform Jews, Sunni Muslims, Hindus, Buddhists, and others could become parts of particularistic instruments. The thousands of observable reflectors of SWB make it possible to develop numerous indexes to "measure" the various multidimensional aspects of spirituality. If all validly reflect SWB, they should be intercorrelated, as indeed they are in exploratory research.[35] Some nursing studies, for example, identify and validate indicators by using the eighteen symptoms that define the nursing diagnosis of Spiritual Distress, "a disruption in the life principle that pervades a person's entire being and that integrates and transcends one's biologic and psychosocial nature."[36] Is this the same ailment as Teasdale's "spiritual deprivation?"[37] He indicates that the elderly are in that state when they are made to feel useless, ashamed of their age, alienated for being unproductive, and devoid of purpose because civilization has lost its spiritual focus. Whether the locus of the problem is interpreted as the individual or society makes a great difference in research, analysis, diagnosis, and treatment.[38]

There are at least two major paradigmatic orientations to spiritual wellness and maturity. One centers around explicit development of the self. It dominates perspectives of the human potential movement, New Age thought, many Eastern religions and new sects, and humanistic psychology. A well-known representative of this approach is Maslow's self-actualization theory with stages of development through which people move to satisfy their needs.[39] Theoretical orientations like this easily become narcissistic, making their disciples "selfish, self-centered elitists" who are "exclusively concerned with their own needs."[40] (Yet Maslow later indicated that self-actualizing people are also "great improvers and reformers of society," integrating self-improvement and social zeal.)[41] Borelli's summary about spiritual orientations and fulfillment in aging reflects this self-centered philosophy: "Ideally, the goal of life is to know oneself, to reach the immortality within, and to integrate oneself spiritually. . . . Jung identified the self as the image of God within everyone. . . . Re-centering on the self is a result of coming to know it through its images."[42]

The other paradigm is directly opposite. It views serving others and "loss of self" as the means for attaining self-fulfillment and spiritual maturity. It is exemplified best by Jesus, who said that he came to give fullness of life to all who accept it as a free gift of God's grace. The way to save one's life is to deny oneself, take up one's cross daily, and follow him, "For whoever wants to save his life will lose it, but whoever loses his life for me will save it" (Luke 9:24). He taught his followers to love others by deeds of kindness and service, not merely feelings and attitudes, as well as to love God and oneself.

These two models of the road to spiritual maturity and wholeness are reflected in contrasts between authentic and inauthentic expressions of spirituality[43] and in the I-E concept to distinguish extrinsically oriented persons who *use* religion for selfish ends from the intrinsically oriented who *live* it as the master motive for life.[44] Considerable research has demonstrated significant differences between people of the two orientations.[45] The extrinsic has two major subtypes, the personal-extrinsic oriented toward desires for relief, protection, and comfort, and the social-extrinsic aiming at social rewards from religious participation and activities.[46] To be sure, the motivations are intermingled; intrinsic people do obtain personal and social rewards which, seen in isolation, might lead an observer to consider them as extrinsic.

The Bible emphasizes the importance of being intrinsically oriented to God through faith in Jesus Christ, but far too many who claim the label of "Christian" are extrinsically oriented, trying to earn fulfillment and salvation through "works of righteousness" rather than by accepting God's gift and then in gratitude sharing his love through serving others. Not only hypocrisy, but wars, crusades, persecutions, other conflicts, and hate-mongering among "Christians," can be traced in large part to the greed and selfishness of those with only a superficial commitment. Their "Christian" identity may be only from being born in a "Christian nation," an ascribed status assigned at birth, or a product of social pressures that compelled them to go through a ritual of "being saved" or joining a church. These can be far removed from the genuine commitment associated with intrinsic religiosity.[47] Similar problems of nominal membership and failure to conform to norms plague all the ethical religions.

Critiques indicate that self-centeredness affronts the majesty of God, is a major source of much suffering, and implicitly rejects God's sole title to glory.[48] It frustrates cooperation that transcends the limitations of life through care for others and for the world, and it sinks one into stagnating self-preoccupation.[49] In contrast, "The spirituality of *old age* is characterized by care and wisdom."[50] The biblical perspective is that the *direction* of a life, not its duration, is decisive for its quality.[51] Fullness of life can be a present possession transcending physical condition, but "If we try to save ourselves, we self-destruct. . . . To be selfish, turned in upon oneself, guarantees failure."[52] "The central core of Christianity is selflessness, not self-centeredness."[53] Wholeness is possible only by intrinsically experiencing death to all that dehumanizes others and oneself.[54]

OTHER SIGNIFICANT ISSUES

There are divergent viewpoints about many other topics related to spirituality and wholeness. One is the "life after life" accounts of pleasant experiences during clinical death.[55] Rawlings, an instructor of resuscitation in medical schools, found that only about twenty percent of all who are revived volunteer any experience in a life beyond death's door; generalizing to all deaths from one-fifth is a bad error. Worse yet, about half recount horrible experiences immediately upon recovery, yet when questioned only a few hours later have so strongly suppressed them that they cannot be recalled, much less recounted even to friends and family.

> No one cares to admit his failures in this life; and certainly no one wants to admit his being in hell in the life beyond. . . . The authors of the earlier books on life-after-death experiences are all psychologists or psychiatrists who have not personally resuscitated *any* of the people they have discussed in their books. They interview other doctors' patients, sometimes days, weeks, or even years following the clinical death episode. They interrogate volunteers. Volunteers report good experiences, not "bad" ones. . . . Now we are finding just as many hell experiences as heavenly ones among these revived patients.[56]

Wishful thinking, rejection of "unpleasant" Bible teachings about the afterlife, and belief in reincarnation are among the sociopsychological and theological sources of divergent ideas about human death, dying, and ultimate destiny. To my knowledge, no social or behavioral scientist has conducted comparative research on the subject, but I am sure that people's ideas about the afterlife are very significant to their conduct and sense of well-being.[57] Spiritual needs certainly are present when one is dying; "While spiritual well-being is important throughout life, it is particularly important as one faces death."[58]

Even in well-intended services by religious agencies, it is easy to make recipients "objects of charity when they are only asking for their just due."[59] The demeaning occurs in part from confusing law and gospel, justice and love. "People are encouraged to bolster their self-esteem and feather their nest in heaven with grandiose gifts of benevolence, instead of shouldering a just burden of taxation which will guarantee to each member of society those basic requirements necessary for human life."[60]

Concepts of the essential nature of humanity greatly influence thinking and conduct as well. The ancient Greek dualistic perspective that viewed the body as evil and the spirit or inner core of the person as inherently good but imprisoned within an evil body still influences much of Western civilization. One consequence of such belief is that "True spirituality is seen to be the release of the spirit from the body. This dualist view leads to a low regard for human life. . . . Since only the spirit matters, the body is either scorned or considered irrelevant."[61] Again, I know of no research directly analyzing the consequences of diverse perspectives on human nature for wholeness in the later years.

In the desire to be "ecumenical," to affirm religious liberty, to honor individual differences, and to respect divergent ideologies and faiths by "therapeutic neutrality," many are caught in a trap of relativism. They imply that it is important to have faith regardless of its content and object, that every form of spirituality is equally valid, and that they should avoid sharing the spiritual resources that nourish their own souls lest they be accused of proselytising or manipulating others. They are easily caught up in a "vertigo of relativity" by which "a kind of skepticism develops when one encounters one system of meaning after another and they all seem plausible. It is the very plausibility of them all that seems to undermine each in turn."[62] Failing to make values clear may actually betray them, injuring those we influence as well as ourselves.

A significant complication in research on spiritual wellness and maturity is the inability to observe them empirically. As with most psychological concepts (alienation, intelligence, motivation, pain, etc.), we can observe only concomitants, correlates, consequences, and self-reports which we can use as indicators. SWB indicators are closely related to the symptoms and signs of mental health and illness, personality integration, meaning in life, and functional social relationships. Is the essence of total well-being so tightly linked with spirituality that separate measurement of its social, psychological, and spiritual dimensions is impossible? NICA's definition of SWB seems to imply that, and a recent analysis of attitude dimensions suggests it, concluding that "there is the possibility of a third unidentified variable influencing both the meaning in life and well-being."[63] It is likely that the most important missing variable is in the spiritual domain.

There is also the danger of reifying SWB measures so that scores are interpreted as the real phenomenon rather than as research constructs or statistical artifacts. Analogously, spiritual formation methods always must be recognized as only means to guide people into a relationship with God, not taken idolatrously as constituting that relationship.[64]

Far too many religious groups serving the aging pay so much attention to empirically observable needs related to health, transportation, food, home services, and social relationships that they fail to minister to spiritual needs in any but the most perfunctory modes. No other agency is expected to make spiritual concerns a primary focus, so when churches and synagogues fail to accentuate spiritual ministries, they betray the people they serve. If trapped by the devastating myth that the elderly cannot learn and change, they reinforce the ageism of contemporary society. They ought instead to nurture spiritual growth in late life, for even the old-old who are bedridden can continue to develop spiritually.[65]

CONCLUSIONS

All are on a spiritual journey, whether they recognize it or not. Just as the earth is immersed in its atmosphere, humanity is engulfed by the supernatural, the "true life" behind the life that is lived outwardly in relationship to other people. "The supernatural is not made a separate section of social life, something juxtaposed to the natural, which individuals may accept or reject at will. . . . society in its complex wholeness . . . is found to exist within the atmosphere of the supernatural."[66] Even those who deny its ontological reality live within it and are spiritual beings. This is sobering, but it also provides hope, the motivation to continue growing spiritually, and an impetus to incorporate spiritual wellness and growth into gerontological theory, research, and practice.

Spiritual maturity cannot be attained in isolation. However expressed, it involves an ongoing process of relational interdependence between God, self, and others, not merely independence or dependence.[67] There can be neither a self-made person nor anyone genuinely fulfilled or "whole" except as a person-in-community, sharing identity, experiences, goals, nourishment, and interactive support with others. The Christian symbolism of Communion, in which all share the same bread and wine as emblems of their common source of spiritual life, typifies the wholeness that is possible only through receiving God's free gifts of grace and then going out to serve as different parts of the same body directed by the divine head, Jesus Christ. The *anamnesis* of creatively remembering past events of God's guidance is a closely related aspect of the life review that can nourish spiritual growth in the later years.[68] Helping people to "harvest past experiences" is an important spiritual resource.[69] Even burdens and losses can become means for quality aging and spiritual gain.[70]

Evidence is accumulating to indicate that SWB is a significant source of psychological well-being and is both a meliorating and therapeutic force in physical health.[71] During the "sabbath" stage of life it provides refreshment, inspiration, renewal, and growth, moving the aging and elderly into an ever deeper experience of wholeness, peace, and spiritual well being or *shalom*.[72] Far beyond the psychological subjectivism of mere "feelings of well-being," it involves peace with God, others, and oneself.

Yet one is never completely mature in this life, at least within Christianity, for nobody fully conforms to all ideals. "If we claim to be without sin, we deceive ourselves and the truth is not in us" (1 John 1:8). The quest for wholeness, theologically the same as that for holiness, is a lifelong developmental task.[73] Christian maturity is a call; it is never complete in this life, for death is part of the treatment as Christians — "saints in therapy" — mature.[74]

NOTES

1. Kenneth Leech, "The Soul and the Social Order," *Weavings* 1(2,1986):6.

2. David O. Moberg, *Spiritual Well-Being: Background and Issues* (Washington, DC: White House Conference on Aging, 1971), p. 3.

3. White House Conference on Aging, *Section Recommendations on Spiritual Well-Being* (Washington, DC: Government Printing Office. 1971).

4. Vincent John Fecher (Compiler), *Religion and Aging: An Annotated Bibliography*. San Antonio, Texas: Trinity University Press, 1982).

5. See Craig C. Thorburn (Compiler and Annotator), *A Bibliography on Spirituality and Aging* (Toronto: Canadian Institute of Religion and Gerontology, n.d., ca.1984), and Richard Fehring and Ruth Stollenwerk, *Bibliography on Spirituality and Nursing Care* (Milwaukee, Wis.: Marquette University College of Nursing, 1987).

6. Barbara P. Payne, "Religious Life of the Elderly: Myth or Reality?," in *Spiritual Well-Being of the Elderly*, ed. James A. Thorson and Thomas C. Cook Jr. (Springfield, Ill.: Charles C. Thomas, 1980), pp. 221-224.

7. David Hay, *Exploring Inner Space: Scientists and Religious Experience* (New York: Penguin Books, 1982), pp. 210-211.

8. Sheldon S. Tobin, James W. Ellor, and Susan M. Anderson-Ray, *Enabling the Elderly: Religious Institutions Within the Community Service System* (Albany: State University of New York Press, 1986).

9. Princeton Religion Research Center, *Religion in America 1982* (Princeton, N.J.: The Gallup Poll, 1982).

10. Arthur N. Schwartz, Cherie L. Snyder, and James A. Peterson, *An Introduction to Gerontology*, 2nd ed. (New York: Holt, Rinehart and Winston, 1984), p. 228, and David O. Moberg, "The Ecological Fallacy: Concerns for Program Planners," *Generations* 8(1,1983):12-14.

11. David O. Moberg and Patricia M. Brusek, "Spiritual Well-Being: A Neglected Subject in Quality of Life Research," *Social Indicators Research* 5(1978):303-323, and Moberg, 1983.

12. See Wesley Pippert, "The Moral Dimension of the News," *His*, 38(5,1978):29-31, and Editorial, "If God Held a Press Conference," *Christianity Today*, 26(10,1982):12-13.

13. Richard A. Kalish, "The New Ageism and the Failure Models: A Polemic," *The Gerontologist*, 19(1979):398-402.

14. David O. Moberg, ed., *Spiritual Well-Being: Sociological Perspectives* (Washington, D.C.: University Press of America, 1979).

15. David O. Moberg, "Subjective Measures of Spiritual Well-Being," *Review of Religious Research*, 25(1984):351-364.

16. Susan H. McFadden, "Attributes of Religious Maturity in Aging People," *Journal of Religion and Aging*, 1(3,1985):39-48.

17. Frederick S. Walz, "Halfistic?: A Challenge to Wholistic Health Centers," *Wholistic Wellspring*, 1(1,1980):5-7.

18. William M. Peterson, ed., *Handbook of the Wholistic Medical Practice* (Hinsdale, Ill.: Wholistic Health Centers, 1981).

19. Melvin A. Kimble, "Education for Ministry with the Aging." in *Ministry with the Aging*, ed. William M. Clements (San Francisco: Harper & Row, 1981), pp. 211-212; see also David O. Moberg, *Wholistic Christianity* (Elgin, Ill.: Brethren Press, 1985).

20. Leech, p. 9.

21. George A. Lane, S.J., *Christian Spirituality An Historical Sketch* (Chicago: Loyola University Press, 1984), pp. 74-76.

22. Robert T. Sears, S.J., "Afterword," in *Christian Spirituality*, ed. George A. Lane, S.J. (Chicago: Loyola University Press, 1984), p. 79.

23. Ibid., p. 80.

24. Frank C. Senn, ed., *Protestant Spiritual Traditions* (Mahwah, N.J.: Paulist Press, 1986), p. 6.

25. Adrian van Kaam, ed., "Spiritual Formation: Contemporary Jewish Perspectives," *Studies in Formative Spirituality*, 8(1987):1-144.

26. David O. Moberg, "Is Your Church an Honest Ally or a Friendly Foe of the Aged?" *Journal of Christian Education* 3(1,1982):51-64.

27. Charles H. Mindel and C. Edwin Vaughan, "A Multidimensional Approach to Religiosity and Disengagement," *Journal of Gerontology* 33(1978): 103-108.

28. David O. Moberg, "Spirituality, Aging, and Spiritual Care," in *Well-Being and the Elderly: An Holistic View*, ed. Geralyn Graf Magan and Evelyn L. Haught (Washington, D.C.: American Association of Homes for the Aging, 1986), pp. 11-22.

29. Kalish.

30. Eugene C. Bianchi, *Aging as a Spiritual Journey* (New York: Crossroad Publishing Co., 1984), p. 198.

31. The genesis effect theory with its seven dialectically connected cycles of human and spiritual development is the newest and perhaps the most sophisticated of these (Brian P. Hall, *The Genesis Effect: Personal and Organizational Transformations*. Mahwah, N.J.: Paulist Press, 1986).

32. Although it is oriented to the personal growth of the one making the life review, the best guide to this process is Barbara J. Hateley, *Telling Your Story, Exploring Your Faith* (St. Louis, Mo.: CBP Press, 1985).

33. Schwartz et al.

34. F. Eugene Yates, "Knowing Your Age," *Journal of Religion and Aging* 2(1/2,1985):47.

35. David O. Moberg, "Subjective Measures," pp. 358-359.

36. Mi Ja Kim, Gertrude K. McFarland, and Audrey M. McLane, eds., *Pocket Guide to Nursing Diagnoses* (St. Louis, Mo.: C. V. Mosby Co., 1984), pp. 57-58.

37. Wayne Teasdale, "The Mystical Dimension of Aging," in *Aging: Spiritual Perspectives*, ed. Francis V. Tiso (Lake Worth, Fla.: Opera Pia International, Sunday Publications, 1984), pp. 224-225.

38. I personally cannot conceive of any appropriate way to perceive spirituality as residing in society at large, although the spiritual orientations and lives of persons invariably are greatly and reciprocally influenced by social forces, so we must not ignore them.

39. Abraham Maslow, *Motivation and Personality* (New York: Harper & Row, 1954), and *Religions, Values, and Peak Experiences* (New York: Penguin Books, 1976).

40. Hateley, p. 30.

41. Abraham Maslow, "Comments on 'Religions, Values, and Peak Experiences,'" in *Psychology and Religion*, ed. Margaret Gorman (Mahwah, N.J.: Paulist Press, 1985), p. 305.

42. John Borelli, "The Paradigm of Aging," in *Aging: Spiritual Perspectives*, ed. Francis V. Tiso (Lake Worth, Fla.: Opera Pia International, Sunday Publications, 1982), pp. 192-193.

43. Edward Kinerk, S. J., "Toward a Method for the Study of Spirituality," in *Psychology and Religion: A Reader*, ed. Margaret Gorman (Mahwah, N.J.: Paulist Press, 1985), pp. 320-324.

44. Gordon W. Allport and J. M. Ross, "Personal Religious Orientation and Prejudice," *Journal of Personality and Social Psychology* 5(1967):423-443.

45. See Michael J. Donahue, "Intrinsic and Extrinsic Religiousness: Review and Meta-analysis," *Journal of Personality and Social Psychology* 48(1985):400-419; Richard D. Kahoe, "The Development of Intrinsic and Extrinsic Religious Orientations," *Journal for the Scientific Study of Religion* 24(1985):408-412; Joyce E. Park and W. Mack Goldsmith, "Values in Persons with Intrinsic, Extrinsic and Quest Religious Orientations," paper presented at Western Division, Christian Association for Psychological Studies, San Diego, Calif., June 22, 1985.

46. Lee A. Kirkpatrick, "A Psychometric Analysis of the Allport-Ross and Feagin Measures of Intrinsic and Extrinsic Religious Orientation," *Research in the Social Scientific Study of Religion*, vol. 1, ed. Monty L. Lynn and David O. Moberg (Greenwich, Conn.: JAI Press, 1988, in press).

47. Nominal or extrinsic religiosity probably is a major source of the anti-Christian bias that is so common among the intelligentsia and professional leaders of contemporary western civilization.

48. Jose Pereira, "A Christian Theology of Aging," in *Aging: Spiritual Perspectives*, ed. Francis V. Tiso (Lake Worth, Fla.: Opera Pia International, Sunday Publications, 1982), pp. 151, 153.

49. Don S. Browning, "Preface to a Practical Theology of Aging," in *Toward a Theology of Aging*, ed. Seward Hiltner (New York: Human Sciences Press, 1975), pp. 162-165.

50. Nathan R. Kollar, "Towards a Spirituality of Aging and Old Age," *Journal of Religion and Aging* 1(3,1985):58.

51. Frank Stagg, *The Bible Speaks on Aging* (Nashville: Broadman Press, 1981).

52. Ibid., pp. 187-188.

53. Ann Vinson, "The Role of Religion in the Maturation of the Autonomous Older Adult," in *Spiritual Well-Being of the Elderly*, ed. James A. Thorson and Thomas C. Cook Jr. (Springfield, Ill.: Charles C. Thomas, 1980), p. 132.

54. Urban T. Holmes, "Worship and Aging: Memory and Repentance," in *Ministry with the Aging*, ed. William M. Clements (San Francisco: Harper & Row, 1981), pp. 91-106.

55. Raymond Moody, *Life After Life* (Covington, Ga.: Mockingbird Books, 1975), and Elisabeth Kuebler-Ross, *On Death and Dying* (New York: Macmillan, 1969).

56. Maurice S. Rawlings, *Before Death Comes* (Nashville: Thomas Nelson, 1980), pp. 21, 187. See also his *Beyond Death's Door* (Nashville: Thomas Nelson, 1978).

57. David O. Moberg, "Spiritual Well-Being of the Dying," in *Aging and the Human Condition*, ed. Gari Lesnof-Caravaglia (New York: Human Sciences Press, 1981), pp. 139-155.

58. Tobin et al., p. 128.

59. Martin J. Heinecken, "Christian Theology and Aging: Basic Affirmations," in *Ministry with the Aging*, ed. William M. Clements (San Francisco: Harper & Row, 1981), pp. 85-86.

60. Ibid., p. 86.

61. Sharon Fish and Judith Allen Shelly, *Spiritual Care: The Nurse's Role*, 2nd ed. (Downers Grove, Ill.: InterVarsity Press, 1983), pp. 31-32.

62. Craig Dykstra and Sharon Parks, eds., *Faith Development and Fowler* (Birmingham, Ala.: Religious Education Press, 1986), p. 4.

63. Gary T. Reker, Edward J. Peacock, and Paul T. P. Wong, "Meaning and Purpose in Life and Well-Being: A Life-Span Perspective," *Journal of Gerontology* 42(1987):49.

64. Tilden Edwards, "Beyond Methods in the Spiritual Life," *Weavings*, 1(1,1986):39-40.

65. Moberg, "Spirituality, Aging . . ."

66. Luigi Sturzo, *The True Life: Sociology of the Supernatural*, trans. Barbara Barclay Carter (London: Geoffrey Bles, 1947), p. 17.

67. Jared Philip Pingleton, "An Integrated Model of Relational Maturity," *Journal of Psychology and Christianity* 3(1984):57-66.

68. Arthur H. Becker, "Pastoral Theological Implications of the Aging Process," *Journal of Religion and Aging* 2(3,1986):29-30; William M. Clements, "Aging and the Dimensions of Spiritual Development," *Journal of Religion and Aging* 2(1/2,1985):127-136; W. Paul Jones, "Aging as a Spiritualizing Process," *Journal of Religion and Aging* 1(1,1984):5-6.

69. Patricia Ross, "Discovering the Spiritual Resources in Aging," *Chicago Theological Seminary Register* 63(4,1973):9; see Hateley; Joseph A. Sittler, "Epilogue: Exploring the Multiple Dimensions of Aging," *Journal of Religion and Aging* 2(1/2,1986):165-172; Gregory D. Gross, "The Spiritual Lifeline: An Experiential Exercise," *Journal of Religion and Aging* 1(3,1985):31-37; Bruce J. Horacek, "Life Review: A Pastoral Counseling Technique," in *Spiritual Well-*

Being of the Elderly, ed. James A. Thorson and Thomas C. Cook Jr. (Springfield, Ill.: Charles C. Thomas, 1980), pp. 100-107.

70. William E. Hulme, "Quality Aging," *Journal of Religion and Aging* 1(2,1984):53-62.

71. Elisabeth McSherry, "The Spiritual Dimension of Elder Health Care," *Generations* 8(1,1986):18-21; David O. Moberg, "Spirituality and Science: The Progress, Problems, and Promise of Scientific Research on Spiritual Well-Being," *Journal of the American Scientific Affiliation*, 38(1986):186-194; George H. Gallup Jr., "To Live a Meaningful Life," *Decision* 28(1,1987):8-9.

72. Robert L. Katz, "Jewish Values and Sociopsychological Perspectives on Aging," in *Toward a Theology of Aging*, ed. Seward Hiltner (New York: Human Sciences Press, 1975), pp. 135-150.

73. Charles J. Fahey, "Spiritual Well-Being of the Elderly in Relation to God," in *Spiritual Well-Being of the Elderly*, ed. James A. Thorson and Thomas C. Cook Jr. (Springfield, Ill.: Charles C. Thomas, 1980), pp. 61-63.

74. Miriam Murphy, *Prayer in Action: A Growth Experience* (Nashville: Abingdon, 1979).

Spiritual Maturity
and Meaning-Filled Relationships:
A Sociological Perspective

Barbara Payne, PhD

SUMMARY. The process of self-development, spiritual maturity and the construction of new meaning-filled relationships in late life are analyzed through the actions and interactions observed in the biographical case history of Sarah-Patton Boyle. Atchley's four stages in the process of retirement applied to the case of Sarah-Patton Boyle identifies the changes in her social roles and relationships and the struggle to maintain a positive self-view in the midst of socio-environmental changes. The struggle to continue "spiritual self" identity and ties with the church are discussed.

Two popular assumptions about older persons are that they become more religious and that role losses accompanying retirement reduce the meaning of their remaining relationships. Research evidence does not support either of these assumptions. Religiosity has been found to be related to period effects, previous religious activity and chronic health problems among the frail elderly.[1] Based on current research Breytspraak reports that not only do people seem to come to terms with their deprived statuses without suffering disintegration of the self but the meaning of these role losses assigned by gerontologists do not coincide with those which older people assign to them.[2]

This paper examines the meaning of relationships and self-development from a symbolic interaction perspective as a framework for understanding "spiritual development or religious growth and

---

Barbara Payne is Director of the Gerontology Center, Georgia State University.

meaning-filled relationships." It discusses the historical background of the problem as the basis for selecting the symbolic interaction perspective; explores some of the basic assumptions of the perspective; illustrates the process of self-development and construction of the meaning of new relationships through the case study of Sarah-Patton Boyle;[3] and discusses the implication for gerontological theory, research and practice.

HISTORICAL BACKGROUND

The earliest interpretations of relationships accompanying aging were based on the withdrawal or disengagement from significant social roles, such as work roles. The withdrawal was viewed as mutually satisfying for individuals and society.

From the disengagement perspective, older persons discard task-oriented, socially functional, interpersonal roles and take on socially unessential or peripheral roles and consummatory roles. This includes a decline in relationships based on love and emotional ties.

The societal definition of who is old and when disengagement begins was set by the enactment of the Social Security Act of 1935. Sixty-five, as the legal age for benefits, became the social age for entering "old age." So prevalent has the chronological age of 65 become as the symbol for "the elderly" that those who do not retire at or before this "appropriate age" are carefully or suspiciously watched for signs of decline, dysfunction or withdrawal. It is common practice for the "near retirement age" employee to experience withdrawal from co-workers as well as exclusion from training and planning functions. That is, there is a prior socialization to the "retired status" that shifts the worker from an aspiring to a declining status.

Consequently, people begin to think of themselves as elderly at or about the age of 65 and experience a change in self-perception and in social relationships. There is also an increased sensitivity to physical or psychological changes that might lead to dependency. As early as 1965, Arnold Rose observed that:

disengagement is by no means voluntary. The older person is pushed out of his occupations, formal and informal associations connected with occupation, and even out of leadership roles in many kinds of non-occupational associations.[4]

Older people were not even valued in unpaid productive work, such as volunteering.

The social invention of mass retirement and the definition of old as 65 years of age resulted in loss of relationships, power and prestige. Retirement was viewed as a "roleless role" and retired persons as not living full "whole" lives made up of relationships filled with social functional meaning.[5]

This was a dismal view. With the passage of the Older Americans Act of 1965 an additional negative view of older persons as a social problem emerged. It reinforced age segregation, the stigma and the isolation of the aged from the rest of society.[6] John Gardner summarized the situation as:

> a cruel and ironic contradiction in the fate of our older citizens. Never before have older people been able to look forward to so many years of vitality; but never have they been so firmly shouldered out of every significant role in life — in the family, in the world of work, and in the community.[7]

Breytspraak points out that most early gerontologists were so dominated by reactions-adaptation and adjustment to the changes in and the denigration of the social status roles of older persons that they were distracted from the older person as an actor with the ability to mediate, reconstruct and maintain identity, purpose and meaning in the midst of change and loss.[8]

Arnold Rose was an exception. He observed that some "elderly" would and were resisting the shift to the new role and negative conceptions; that they would construct an age-group consciousness; and that they would organize their own associations to instill group pride and group identity. He predicted that older people would work together to identify common problems and take social action (individual and organized) to correct the situation. Eventually they would be given a new distinct position.[9] Remember, this view was prior to AARP, Maggie Kuhn, the Gray Panthers, The Older Woman's League, etc.

Rose was also the first gerontologist to apply symbolic interactionist views to aging and to argue:

> that it is possible for the interactional context and process (the environment, the persons and the encounters in it) to significantly affect the kind of aging process a persons will experience and construct.[10]

Most of the early theories and even the more recent adaptation of stratification[11] and exchange theories[12] to aging, are predominately structural-functional perspectives that perpetuate the emphasis on role losses and negative meanings of relationships. Individuals, by virtue of age, lose access to valued social roles with the accompanying loss of power and prestige. This leaves compliance as the role for older persons in relationships.

In contrast, the symbolic interaction perspective views the older person as actively constructing positive relationships with others and society. They are change agents in an aging society.

The search for a theoretical framework for understanding the relationship between spiritual maturity and the construction of meaning-filled relationships has led to an even stronger adherence to a processual and dialectical position. This is a departure from stages or life course development. The processual-dialectical-contextual-now includes the impact that interactions of present and past period effects, cohort memberships, and social change have on social, psychological and physical aspects of aging. Furthermore, it allows for the plasticity of the individual in response to change and development — at *any* age.

Stages are too structured and constricting. Neugarten observed that people are breaking out of defined structures.[13] There is a blurring of age related behavior and the age timing of life events — e.g., marriage, parenting, retiring. There are period effects, such as the golden parachute phenomenon of early retirement of those in their 50s and the reported return of the Baby Boomers and Yuppies to church. If there are stages, they seem not to be linear or organismic — some may not ever occur nor need to as a necessary and sufficient cause of maturity, e.g., marriage, retirement, single careers, parenting.

THE MEANING OF RELATIONSHIPS
AND SELF-DEVELOPMENT:
THE SYMBOLIC INTERACTION PERSPECTIVE

Some of the most explicit thinking on the meaning of relationships and the process of self-development has come out of the symbolic interaction perspective.[14] However, only recently have some gerontologists utilized this perspective to interpret the relationships, meanings and self-concepts of older persons.[15] This perspective is especially appropriate for our purposes, because it is based on a processual view of self-conceptualization and self-development that is operative at any age or stage of the life cycle, including old age.

Since it is not possible nor appropriate to provide a detailed analysis of symbolic interaction in this paper, we will focus on several basic assumptions about the meaning of relationships in late life and how these become the social processes through which a new or changed self emerges. Through a case study we will trace how these relationships construct a new social world. These assumptions include:

1. Only human beings have the capacity for reflective thinking and the utilization of that reflecting for present responses and to chart future directions. This is not to deny biological inheritance and genetic programmed potential, but rather to underscore that, unlike other animals, the human being is instinct-poor and symbol-rich.

This unique psycho-social quality makes self-identity and purpose essential for human life at all ages. Self-identity and life purpose are not assumed to come with biological birth but rather to have evolved out of relationships with others and society in a specific period of history with its unique sets of events, values and norms. It is out of such interaction that self-identity, values and meaning emerge. Spiritual maturity then, as it is used in sociological context, would relate the development of self-identity and purpose in later life as a consequence of the meanings of past and present relationships.

Although obvious changes take place in the aging process, the stress is on the present. Life review for the older person as well as for younger age groups is for enriching and understanding the present. In like manner life previews or "futuring" are for the same purpose.

2. The human individual acts toward things and other human individuals on the basis of the meanings the relationships have for him/her.

3. The meanings of relationships are derived from or arise out of the social interactions the individual has with others. These interactions (our own and others) serve as gestures that become symbols. Symbols indicate the social meaning and definition of one's emotions in relation to given situations such as grief at death, rejection at divorce, joy at success and so on.[16]

4. Meanings are handled and modified through an interpretative reflective process used by the individual in relationships to things and others encountered in the social world. These ideas are developed by Mead from the social-behavioral works of Mead, a behavioral social scientist, and Buber, an existentialist, on the spiritual dimensions, especially from his ideas of the "I-Thou" relationship.[17]

These brief assumptions of symbolic interaction serve as the background for four questions for the case study: (1) what are the interactions involved? This includes the role perceptions and role interactions with significant others in the individual's social circle. (2) What are the symbolic meanings of these relationships? These meanings apply to the actor as well as the significant others. (3) What are the changes in these interactions and their meanings over time in the case study?; and (4) what are the implications for older persons in terms of the social self and symbolic meanings?

SARAH-PATTON BOYLE: A CASE STUDY

The process of self-development, spiritual maturity and the construction of new meanings in late life is best understood as it is observed operative in the action and interactions of specific individuals in their social settings or circles. For this reason we have chosen the case of Sarah-Patton "Patty" Boyle as she ends one stage of her life and moves into the last stage.[18]

For purpose of analysis Atchley's four stages in the process of retirement are adapted for the analysis of four specific stages in Patty's process of self-development and new role construction: (1) the retirement event; (2) the honeymoon; (3) depression, disengagement and despair; and (4) new self-construction and meanings.[19]

Stage 1: The Retirement Event

When Patty Boyle retired at age 60 she was a respected and competent college professor in Charlottesville, Virginia; honored for her prominent role in the southern civil rights movement; a wife of 33 years; a mother of adult children and a committed church person. She had a strong self-image and knew what she wanted from the rest of her life — to bring into full function the person she was created to be. She felt she was moving toward such fulfillment.

She described her feelings about this point in her life as experiencing "a strong outward thrust of accumulated wisdom and practical know-how. I expected to reap a good harvest by using them. A future was out there waiting. It didn't occur to me that I might not be able to deal with it."[20]

Stage 2: The Honeymoon

The honeymoon period of Patty's retirement begins with a mixture of positive and negative events and feelings. Her expectations of a closer relationship with her husband were dashed by his sudden announcement that he was leaving. Their marriage was over. Despite her hurt, she maintained a positive attitude; she resolved to focus not on what she had lost, but on what she would gain — a new freedom and independence.

She thrust herself into a new and totally different physical and social environment. She moved from being a home owner in a college town to an apartment renter in the suburbs of Washington, D.C., and from a mountain view to a rooftop asphalt parking lot view with a few token trees. She ignored the negatives in the physical environment and focused on the few trees and the positive stimuli of a new environment. What she found was that the removal of roles and responsibilities that seemed limiting were not as limiting as having no responsibility to significant others. Freedom from responsibility and from relationships with significant others impeded creativity more than overwork and a tight schedule. *Still,* she clung to a positive self-view, she would act to control and structure a new role, but all relationships were *new* and had to be renegotiated with people who did not see "Patty," but rather a single, older woman.

The choice of a church was symbolic of her decision for a new free life — a place for the new and old to blend. She acted out her self-view as a creative liberal and chose an ecumenical, well-known Washington church rather than one of her own denomination.

Within the church all the newness and change she had chosen led to reminiscence about the changes she had experienced in the past and their meanings for the present newness and change. She began to feel like she had alien status in a strange land.

In the midst of all the new relations — interactions that were mirroring a "Patty" she did not know — she needed one area of stability, one unaltered link to the past — her denominational church. The move to a church of her denomination met her need for shared meanings, rituals and a church family. She found friendliness, self-recognition, group identity, and a feeling that she was needed.

However, Patty's self-identity slowly began to change. She was being treated differently within the church and in all social interactions in a phony, condescending and overly solicitous manner. Some acted toward her as though she was economically, physically and psychologically deficient. These interactions with new "others" made her feel that something must be wrong with her; she felt denigrated. Her identity was spoiled as she learned she was one of those "oldpeople" (spelled one word) and not the creative, exciting, competent, outgoing Patty. The honeymoon was over.

Stage 3: Depression, Disengagement, Despair

Everything in Patty's world had a different appearance. In her words "the discovery that I was old demanded I change my conception of how others saw me as well as how I saw myself and my future. My future would now be dictated by old age."[21]

After a few months of retreating (disengaging), Patty sought once more to establish close working relationships with her church members. Surely in her church she thought:

> no matter how dislocated and destructive the months and years ahead might be, in the home and family of my church I would have an area of solidarity, permanence, strength and eternal belonging. Outside losses would be cushioned by the shared worship of an unchanging God.[22]

This was not to be. The secular negative symbols of the aged were in her church. Older people were viewed as complacently powerful, as an obstruction to progress, as liabilities and/or the object of charitable do-gooder actions.

The final blow for Patty was the liberal theological attack on traditional Christianity by the "God is dead" movement. When she could not accept it or questioned it, she was rebuffed by her pastor and the younger adult leaders. She was abandoned by her church friends. Now it was not just feeling old but seeing herself as having no life ahead, no adventure fulfillment, or accomplishments but just more and more losses — an outsider in her own church. Her church had dumped her. The one place and area of life where she had felt she belonged, the one area of continuity, stability and acceptance was no more. She felt helplessness and betrayal, as though she was falling apart. Disengagement and deep depression settled in and lasted for over four years.

Stage 4: New Self-Construction, Meanings and Relationships

In her deep despair, lost faith in the clergy, alienation from the church, and feeling that her faith was dead, Patty had an experience that began new relations with God and others which created a new self-view. She cried out in her pain, "God help me," but she heard nothing but silence. The unbearable heaviness did not lift. To break the awful silence, she turned on the television. A representative of Alcoholics Anonymous was explaining the use of St. Francis' Serenity prayer as a key to recovery. This prayer, a well known faith symbol, "God Grant me the serenity to accept the things I cannot change, the courage to change the things I can and the wisdom to know the difference," became the turning point. She accepted her feelings of being old, tired, lost and with no hope. She accepted others views of old people as a nuisance, an impediment and not a resource in the church, and her desire to die. This was the starting point. The I-thou relationship was renewed. There was the certainty — God was still there — caring and helping.

The restructuring of the self began with the identification of her most devastating losses — a sense of progress, of contributing, of belonging and of loving and being loved. She tackled these with *action* one by one.

For progress, she enrolled in continuing education classes and workshops to acquire new attitudes, understanding, knowledge and skills. She learned about cars, philosophy, psychology, theology, creative writing, etc. She found stereotypes about the older learners in the classroom, but she could change this by making the highest grade in her class and rid herself of an aging stereotype.

This new view of herself was followed by other community experiences and the establishment of new relationships in which the new Patty acted in jury duty, as a general volunteer at her church, and as a volunteer visitor to retirement homes and nursing homes. Positive feelings about herself and others emerged. The focus was on *now*, not yesterday or tomorrow. She learned to help her peers (other older people) by confirming the person, not directing them; she learned the art of listening. These relationships had deep meaning for Patty, but there were no close significant others. This was the final act of self-development and change. She became the caregiver for an 82-year-old cousin with Alzheimer's disease; she developed significant other relationships with dying persons and their families. Patty, the "new" Patty, emerged as a person who understood physical losses, disease, dying and death, grief, and how to give help and receive help. In giving love, she received love to live in the now and not fear the future in which she knew the Holy One (the Thou) was/would be present. Progress? Spiritual maturity? Relationships filled with significant positive and negative meanings? This was preparation for the final event, her own dying and death.

REFLECTIONS AND IMPLICATIONS:
THEORETICAL, METHODOLOGICAL
AND PRACTICE

As you will note it has been possible through the case study to identify role relationships, meanings and changes. These were decisive for Patty in her struggle toward self-fulfillment (maturity) and meaningful relations. The four stages in her retirement story reflect changes in her as "actor" and in significant relationships to others. Through these stages she was in a struggle with the "thingification" of herself as "olderperson spelled one word," of others as contributors to the negative image and the efforts at "Thouification" of significant relationships. That is, she was caught in a struggle to maintain her self-view in the process of life stage and socio-environmental changes and at the same time to continue her "spiritual self" in relation to/with the church.

In any case, it is clear that the symbolic interaction perspective provides fruitful insights into the dramatic changes which took place in Patty's life. It is obvious that Atchely's four stages in the process of retirement are considerably enriched by reviewing them within the symbolic interaction framework.

From a social scientist perspective spiritual maturity was treated in the Median tradition of the self as actor in religious roles and in relation with significant others in the religious social context—the organized church. Religious others, religious beliefs, rituals and practices of the church were treated as the generalized other that constituted a significant part of Patty's self view.

The limitations to the symbolic interaction perspective are most evident in efforts to explain the God or Thou relationship. For our purposes the social science symbolic interactionist is limited by its humanistic basis. It is at this point that we need to identify the contribution that relational philosophers and theologians could make to a theoretical development in the study of spiritual maturity and the meaning of relationships. Specifically, I would suggest drawing upon the triadic relational model of Josiah Royce and the significance he places on the "third" in the development of the social self and community, his concept of the beloved community and loyalty.[23] Since Royce influenced Richard Neibuhr, the relational theologian, we would profit from a review of his development of relationships.[24] These would be in addition to Buber's understanding of interaction being "truly human" and true community as based on mutual relations with God and then with one another.

Chappel and Orbach point out that we know little about how the past is remembered, and reconstruction is done from the more than reminiscent perspective of the present.[25] Furthermore, social scientists seldom study the remembered past in terms of what it can tell us about the present situation of an older person. In the case of Patty we observed her use of her past experiences and relations in the church as a sources of continuity in the midst of change. When this perceived stable relationship with its symbolic meanings — rituals, the building itself, traditional (past) beliefs are called into question, she cannot deal with her present situation. She eventually reconstructs elements of the meanings of past religious experiences in the present through new social roles and relationships: the volunteer with other older people; through the family caregiver role; and through being with significant others who are dying.

Methodology

To study the changes in behavior of older persons — their roles and the meanings of these roles — social scientists need to ask different questions and utilize retrospective qualitative methods, such as oral histories or autobiographies (e.g., Boyle), that use guided questions about the past roles and their meaning in relation to past roles and their current meaning. The use of participant observation or an adaptation of the focus group used in marketing research to observe the negotiation of meanings and rearranging of goals in process would provide new understanding of changes which influence the aging experience. Such research could provide a view of older persons as dynamic individuals, experiencing self development and constructing new societal meanings of old behavior.

Breytspraak observes that "we need to know more about self-concepting — not just *the* self concept."[26] That is, how do older people come to characterize themselves in certain ways, e.g., Patty's self-concept, as seeking fulfillment? How do people at any age change these characteristics?

Researchers need to study the differences that being in a particular cohort makes to self-concepting and change; what difference do specific events or movements have on self-concepting and changes in life-span development, especially in late life? For example, the "God is dead" theological movement of the early 1960s forced changes in Patty's self concepting and the meaning of her relationships. What is it in the 1980s that forces changes in the self and other views of older persons — and the meaning of roles: negative forces, such as problems of healthcare costs, stereotypes of older persons as bad drivers with too much money and power; positive views of older persons as vigorous, free and having resources.

Practice

In terms of professionals and other institutional members, the case of Patty indicates the need for a deeper understanding and appreciation of the dynamic plasticity of the self — even into old age; that self-development and changes do occur. They must also understand and appreciate the significance that the symbolic meanings of the church as a family — the beliefs, rituals and practices — have for older persons. Such an understanding could provide direction in counseling older persons, in affirming their personhood, and in helping older persons find new, appropriate and contributing roles in the church. It may be that the greatest spiritual growth occurs as one struggles with physical losses and dying. We know very little about this late growth experience from older persons.

At the very least, the professions need increased sensitivity to the insults of ageism within the church and the practices of professionals, to be aware of the struggles of older persons, socially and spiritually, and to be there for them.

I am reminded that all beginnings are endings and all endings are beginnings. I hope for you, as it is for me, that the end of this review is the beginning of new theoretical perspectives, the utilization of new research approaches and new directions for practice.

NOTES

1. Blazer, D.G. & Palmore, E. "Religion and Aging in a Longitudinal Panel." *The Gerontologist*, 1976, 16(1), pp.82-85.

2. Breytspraak, M. *The Development of Self in Later Life*. Boston: Little Brown & Co., 1984; Cottrel, L.S., Jr. and Atchley, R.C. "Women in Retirement: A Preliminary Report." Oxford, OH: Scripps Foundation, 1969; George L.K. *Role Transition in Later Life*. Monterey, CA.: Brooks/Dole, 1980.

3. Boyle, Sarah-Patton. *The Desert Blooms*. Nashville: Abingdon Press, 1983.

4. Rose, A.M. "The Subculture of the Aging: A Framework for Research in Social Gerontology." In Rose, A.M., Peterson, W.A. (Eds.). Older People and Their Social World. Philadelphia: Davis, 1965, pp.3-16.

5. Burgess, E.W. "Personal and Social Adjustments in Old Age." In J.D. Brown, C. Kerr, and E.E. Witte, (Eds.). *The Aged and Society*. Champaign, IL: Industrial Relations Research Association, 1950, pp.138-156.

6. Estes, C.L. *The Aging Enterprise*. San Francisco: Jossey-Bass Publishers, 1979.

7. Gardner, J. *No Easy Victories*. New York: Harper & Row, 1968.

8. Breytspraak, M. 1984, op. cit.

9. Rose, A.M. "A Systemic Summary of Symbolic Interaction Theory." In Rose A.M., (Ed.). *Human Behavior and Social Processes: An Interactionist Approach*. Boston, MA: Houghton, Mifflin, 1962.

10. Rose, A.M. 1962, op. cit.

11. Riley, M.W. "Age Strata in Social System." In R. Binstock and E. Shanas (Eds.). *Handbook of Aging and the Social Sciences*. New York: Van Nostrand Reinhold, 1972; Riley, M.W. "A Sociology of Stratification." In M.W. Riley, M. Johnson, M. and A. Foner, (Eds.). Volume 3, *Aging and Society*. New York: Basic Books, 1972; Dowd, J.J. *Stratification Among the Aged*. Monterey, CA: Brooks/Cole, 1980.

12. Dowd, J.J. "Aging as Exchange: A Preface to a Theory." *Journal of Gerontology*, 1975, 30, pp.584-594.

13. Neugarten, B. An interview in *Psychology Today*, May, 1987.

14. Goffman, E. *Stigma: Notes on the Management of Spoiled Identify*. Englewood Cliffs, NJ: Prentice Hall, 1965; Mead, G.H. *Mind, Self and Society*. Chicago: University of Chicago Press, 1934; Rose, A.M., 1962 and 1965, op. cit.; Goffman, E. *Encounters: Two Studies in the Sociology of Interaction*. Indianapolis IN: Bobs/Merrill, 1961; Goffman, E. *The Presentation of the Self in Everyday Life*. Garden City, NY: Doubleday Anchor Books, 1959; Pfuetze, P.E. *The Social Self*. New York: Bookman Associates, 1954.

15. Brewer, Earl. "Research in Religion and Aging—An Unlikely Scenario." In *Journal of Religion and Aging*. Summer, 1987; Chappell, N.C. and Orbach, H.L. "Socialization in Old Age: A Median Perspective." In V.W. Marshall, (Ed.). *Later Life*. Beverly Hills: Sage Publications, 1987, pp.75-106; Mutran, B. & Reitzes, D. "Intergenerational Support Activities and Well Being

Among the Elderly: Convergence of Exchange and Symbolic Interaction Perspectives." *American Sociological Review*, 1984, 29, pp.117-130; Mutran, B. & Reitzes, D. "Retirement, Identity and Well Being: Realignment of Role Relationships." *Journal of Gerontology*, 1981, 36, pp.733-740; Spense, D.L. "Some Contributions of Symbolic Interaction to the Study of Growing Old." In V.M. Marshall, (Ed.). *Later Life*. Beverly Hills: Sage Publications, 1987, pp.106-124.

16. Chappel, N.C. & Orbach, H.L., 1987, op. cit.

17. Duber, M. *I and Thou* (2nd ed.) New York: Charles Scribner's Sons, 1958; Mead, 1934, op. cit.

18. Boyle, Sarah-Patton, 1983, op. cit., p.30.

19. Atchley, R.C. *The Sociology of Retirement*. Cambridge, MA: Schenkman, 1976.

20. Boyle, Sarah-Patton, 1983, op. cit., p.20.

21. Boyle, Sarah-Patton, 1983, op. cit., p.80.

22. Boyle, Sarah-Patton, 1983, op. cit., p.89.

23. Royce, Josiah. *The Philosophy of Loyalty*. New York: MacMillan, 1914; Royce, Josiah. *Sources of Religious Insight*. New York: Charles Scribner & Sons, 1912.

24. Neibur, H.R. *Christ and Culture*. New York: Harper and Brothers, 1951.

25. Chappel, N.C. & Orbach, H.L., 1987, op. cit.

26. Breytspraak, M., 1984, op. cit.

Spiritual Maturity
in Psychological Development

James E. Birren, PhD

SUMMARY. A review of data from an international survey of life satisfaction in 13 countries indicates that acceptance of the conditions of life increases with age. In relation to religious orientation, in all countries women expressed more adherence to the belief systems of the country than did men. This paper raises the question of change in orientation in the latter portion of life, from a logical analytical perspective to a more subjective one. The search for meaning in the later years would thus appear to have a different focus than for persons in the work years of life.

There is a clear need to explore some of the pathways to maturity and wholeness, both spiritual and psychological in contemporary society. If the elderly are not attaining a sense of meaning or wholeness in their lives, what prospects are there for the young?

There is a difference in emphasis between the activities that comprise religion and those of the behavioral and social sciences. In psychology, the stress is on finding out how life *is lived* rather than on how it *should be lived*. Discussions about religion and maturity move between these two poles: what is characteristic about eldering and elderhood, and what should be characteristic about the second half of life. It is my intention to stay closer to descriptions of *what is* characteristic of the elderly rather than to *what should be*. This does not preclude exploring subjective issues of aging, for matters of mood as well as fantasy can be studied as productively as well as how much money older persons have in their pockets. The interior subjective space of being elderly is the present focus.

James E. Birren is Professor and Brookdale Distinguished Scholar at the University of Southern California.

Bianchi in his book, *Aging as a Spiritual Journey*, uses the term *interiority* to refer to the inner awareness that involves concerns, focus and emotional climate.[1] His interpretation of relevant research literature is that older persons, particularly men, move from active concern with the outside world, to a more internal occupation, "Thus the three main traits are interiority, passivity, and concern for personal satisfaction."[1]

McFadden ties the concept of religious maturity to personal experience and the past. "Religious maturity . . . requires that an individual value the insights and experiences of the past while not remaining bound to the earlier interpretations of the transcendent or of religious symbols, myths and rituals."[2]

Let me say that two features of the many studies of personality stand out in my opinion. The first is that stability rather than change characterizes the adult personality in the second half of life. The other generally accepted finding is that individuals tend to move from extroversion toward introversion. The stability of the adult personality lends itself to the interpretation that in general we become more like ourselves with advancing age. However, the shift of focus would seem to be more inward than outward. A shift toward an interior focus lends itself to a more spiritual outlook in the later years. I would like to see more empirical studies on "the interior life" of older adults.

Joseph Sittler, a Chicago theologian, says: "Purely empirical research is tempted to be contemptuous of the kind of reflective research required by the facts of human aging."[4] He goes on to say: "If there is such a thing as an internal drama of aging, what are the data for which a model must be devised? I would suggest that can never be directly known, but must be intuited by sensitive listening." "I would suggest that the clearest signals to what is the interior life of aging are provided by the aging themselves. The most important drama is the internal testimony."[3]

The interior space of Joseph Sittler is highly relevant. At the 1984 conference on the Church and Aging he was eighty years old and gave a few comments about his personal preoccupations. He said he was giving away his theology books that occupied his attention during his active career and was turning to rereading and adding to the fiction and poetry he read in his youth. Superficially one might interpret these comments as implying that Joseph Sittler the theologian was turning away from religion in his later years. Rather I think he was moving from a logical analytical orientation to an interior emotional or affective focus.

I had a similar discussion with an about-to-retire minister. Like Sittler, he said he was moving away from the analytical theological preoccupations of his early career and days in divinity school toward a more subjective way of looking at life. He believed he was now more accepting of life and differences in people. Both of these individuals portray a move from logic and analysis toward feeling and affect, and I believe, from the way things are organized externally to the way they are experienced internally. The experiences of these two individuals do not provide an instant theory but are suggestive that spirituality in the later years is less focussed on the external formalism of religion and more on the interpretation of life and its feelings.

BACKGROUND

Many years ago, I had two colleagues, Sidney Pressy and Raymond Kuhlen, who were doing research on lifespan development. One of the issues they were concerned with was the place of religion in later adulthood. Data at that time indicated that there was no upward trend with age in church attendance. At the same time, a body of literature suggested that there was a heightened religious concern in the later years. I am prepared to accept the point of view that there is not much change with age in regular church attendance, participation in church sponsored gatherings, and adherence to creed, but there is within individuals a move toward an interior focus of a spiritual character.

The purpose of the National Symposium on Aging held in Zion, Illinois, in September, 1984, was to review the role of the religious sector's activities in the field of aging.[4] While sponsored by the Lutheran Council in the USA, it was broadly oriented with representatives from various religious groups, as well as academic faculty and leaders in social service agencies. From that conference, I strengthened my opinion about the distinction between membership and participation of mature and older adults in churches and their internal spiritual concerns and subjective states. Relevant are conversations I have had with a few elderly intimates who have discussed the fact that they go to church regularly and like to see their friends, but some feel distant or even somewhat alienated from the creed or theology being espoused. Clearly, going to church, meeting friends, and working on projects that grow out of the church is an extension of one's experience and social roles, but it need not reflect a shift in one's spiritual life.

I have come to believe that the inner spiritual life of an individual follows a different life course than does religious behavior or participation. I have the impression that mature and elderly adults seek a wholeness, a meaning in life, that is more integrative of actions and emotions, but less analytical in thought. If such a trend is widely found then explorations of the territory of late life spirituality should be undertaken by both empirical psychologists and students of religion.

STUDY OF AGE AND RELIGION IN CONTEMPORARY SOCIETY

Earlier I mentioned a large international survey on human values and well-being in adult life that was recently published. The total number of people studied was nearly 14,000, with the smallest number of interviews conducted in any country being 981.[5] Measures of four elements of people's outlook on life were derived in the areas of job relations, human relations, materialism, and religiosity. Women showed the strongest belief systems in all countries, which is interesting given the fact that men dominate academic philosophy and theology, as well as the ministry. (See Table 1.)

Other questions were also asked about religiosity, including the belief in a soul, a belief in life after death, a belief that an act of God can save individual souls and society. (See Table 2.)

One of the important features of the survey data is that it shows large differences between nations in beliefs. A dramatic contrast is seen between Japan in which only 7.8% of the population believes in one absolute God, in contrast to 76.1% in the United States. Or, examining the data in the negative sense, 2% of the American population surveyed said no gods existed, in contrast to 21.5% in Japan.

Both Japan and Korea show loose adherence to formal belief systems, yet are highly differentiated societies with high respect for the elderly. (See Table 3.)

Clearly contributing to differences in religious belief are age, gender, and cross-national or cultural differences. Oddly, the United States with its high proportion of fundamental religious belief, is clustered with the countries of the Philippines, India, and Brazil. For the most part, these are developing countries. Countries expressing about 50%, or less, belief in one absolute God are Australia, France, Japan, Singapore, and South Korea. It is strange that the United States on this dimension is closer to developing countries, e.g., Brazil, than it is to Great Britain and West Germany.

Results from the study make it possible to look at cross-national gender differences in views of religion. Of the thirteen nations, the country that shows the largest sex difference in attitudes towards one God is Italy; there the two sexes differ by 23%. The country of the smallest difference is Japan, 1.5%. Rather large in their differences compared to the United States (7.2%) are France with 17.3%, and Great Britain with 18.7%. One may assume that religious belief is bound up in age and gender role differences in these countries.

One striking point in the foregoing is the fact that a belief in monotheism or in atheism has little to do with the conduct of many

Table 1
Belief in one God by males and females in 13 countries [5]
(Source, Leisure Development Center, 1980)

	Male	Female
Australia	46.2	56.1
Brazil	82.6	89.3
Canada	60.7	71.1
France	35.1	52.4
India	71.3	84.0
Italy	51.2	74.2
Japan	7.0	8.5
Philippines	90.4	94.0
Singapore	39.1	46.3
South Korea	23.1	29.5
United Kingdom	7.3	66.0
United States	72.5	79.7
West Germany	46.4	56.6

Table 2
Belief in life after death by males and females in 13 countries[5]
(Source, Leisure Development Center, 1980)

	Percent Male	Female
Australia	53.8	64.6
Brazil	57.6	62.8
Canada	65.4	73.3
France	36.4	50.3
India	54.0	64.5
Italy	41.1	59.4
Japan	46.2	56.7
Philippines	81.4	85.9
Singapore	38.1	41.4
South Korea	45.2	58.8
United Kingdom	40.8	51.3
United States	71.4	76.0
West Germany	44.6	54.2

activities of a society. For example, Japan with 21.5% expression of atheism has about 60% of its older persons living in the household of a child, in contrast to 2% atheistic outlook in America where about 15% of older adults are living with children. Thus, the togetherness of the generations and the veneration between the young and the elderly would appear to be a consequence of different factors than religious belief *per se*.

Belief in one god shows an increase with age throughout the thirteen countries. In the United States, this is somewhat larger for males than for females. Whether this reflects cohort differences and historical periods or ontogenetic change cannot be answered from the data. (See Table 4.)

Of striking interest are the data showing a decline with age in both males and females in a belief in life after death. Does this suggest that the trend toward interiority in late life is not related to a belief in life after death? (See Table 5.)

THE RIB CAME FROM EVE

From an empirical standpoint, the data presented in this paper suggests that women are more traditional in their beliefs than are

Table 3
Proportion of Persons in 13 Countries
Expressing Different Religious Convictions [5]
(Source, Leisure Development Center, 1980)

	No Interview	One God	Many Gods	Not sure but feel God exists	No Gods	N.A.
Australia	1104	50.9	3.6	34.1	7.5	3.9
Brazil	1000	86.0	1.6	9.4	1.9	1.1
Canada	1012	65.9	2.3	25.1	4.8	1.9
France	993	44.2	1.2	31.5	19.3	3.7
India	1000	76.4	12.4	7.4	3.8	0
Italy	1042	62.8	1.5	23.4	6.5	5.8
Japan	1574	7.8	14.5	55.0	21.5	1.2
Philippines	997	92.2	1.8	5.7	0.3	0
Singapore	996	42.7	16.0	35.2	5.7	2.4
South Korea	1006	26.4	3.5	51.1	16.5	2.5
United Kingdom	989	57.2	4.7	21.7	9.7	6.7
United States	1127	76.1	2.4	16.9	2.0	2.6
West Germany	1020	51.9	5.7	24.4	9.6	4.1

47

men. In less than 100 years the strength of man has diminished as a significant factor in our society. At the present time workers control energy, but are no longer sources of energy. It makes little difference whether the male or female finger presses the button to release mammoth energy sources in industry. In the past, the strength of man was an important utility in harvesting, construction of houses and buildings, and the production of heavy industrial goods. Insofar as status and roles were differentiated on the basis of strength, this element has diminished in importance. Thus, the older male, displaced by technology, would seem to have a particular problem in seeking meaning in the late years of life. The reason I have introduced this topic into the discussion has to do with the role of the

Table 4

Belief in one God in the United States by age and sex
(Source, Leisure Development Centers, 1980) [5]

Age	Male	Female
< 29	64.4	75.5
30-39	62.6	73.2
40-49	76.8	83.8
> 50	79.1	85.6

Table 5

Belief in life after death by age and sex in the United States
(Source, Leisure Development Center, 1980) [5]

Percent

Age	Male	Female
< 29	74.1	73.1
30-39	64.8	83.5
40-49	78.0	83.8
> 50	70.1	70.7

power of metaphor in our evolving post-industrial or information society and its impact upon the social thought. What impact has the thought that the rib came from Eve?

One of the themes that strikes me as worthwhile to analyze is the metaphor that the rib came from Adam: that the transmission of power and life came from God to Adam and then to Eve. It occurred to me that from a biological standpoint, men are but differentiated females. The basic genetic traits for both men and women are carried on the X or female chromosome. The dominant sex chromosome in both males and females is the X chromosome. The principal biological difference between a male and a female is the addition of testosterone. The male has a Y chromosome which provides for the synthesis of testosterone, which in turn modifies the expression of the traits carried on the female chromosome.

SUCCESSFUL AGING AND WHOLENESS

The data reported by Butt and Beiser from an international study bear upon the question of whether older individuals are successful in transforming " . . . what might be a final phase of decline and renunciation into one of integrity and integration."[6] In the thirteen country survey there was a rise with age for both men and women in satisfaction with *material needs*. The top countries were South Korea, the Philippines and Japan, and the lowest was India. In terms of satisfaction with *human relations*, the top countries were South Korea, Australia, Italy, and Japan. Unlike these categories, satisfaction with *job relations* reached its peak in the 35-49 year range.

The youngest group, 18-25, was the least satisfied of any age group in terms of overall satisfaction. It also showed the least religiosity. Insofar as the concept of successful aging has some coherence, the data suggest that older adults in most countries are more successful in deriving more contentment in life than are young adults. The fact that older adults do not show much satisfaction with job relations probably reflects the fact that they have relinquished work as a major source of significance in their lives. Individuals over 50 "tend to derive relatively more satisfaction from areas other than work." They are ". . . satisfied with family relationships and neighborhood and are satisfied that their material needs are being met, and they report relatively strong religious beliefs.'' The conclusion of the authors' paper is most pertinent: ''The stereotype that older persons are unhappy with the processes of aging, that they are lonely and isolated, neglected and sick, does not hold true for people in most parts of the world, where to survive is to flourish. Even the very old can and do approach death with a sense of comfort and spiritual well being.'' This is, of course, a broad view of the data which only skims the surface of what we are discussing here.

AUTOBIOGRAPHY, AGING AND SPIRITUALITY

For the past 11 years I have been teaching a graduate course on psychological development through autobiography. I have now collected over 200 autobiographies of men and women, young and old, professional, academic, and lay persons. One of the impressions that has developed in my experience with autobiography is the strength of motivation in mature individuals to obtain an integrated picture of their lives. At another level this might be called the search for meaning. The study of Hedlund,[7] based upon these autobiographies, indicated four main themes in individuals' search for meaning. These are (a) relationships with others, (b) work and career, (c) ideology and religion, and (d) personal development. What is interesting is that the expression of the motivation for obtaining meaning in life through ideology or religion is found in a relatively small proportion of the population. However the thrust toward integration and seeing one's life as a whole does not necessarily have a religious focus for most persons, though it might be judged to be of a spiritual character.

To me there appears to be a psychological dynamism in later life toward interpretation of life, the attainment of some grasp of the essential meaning of one's life as one has lived it. The idea of accounting for one's stewardship of life, and whether one has lived his or her life as expected, appears to concern many people in the later years. Presumably this relates to a sub-theme of later life in terms of the readiness for death.

The literature on aging would suggest that fear of death is not common in older persons. Rather fear of dying is the focus, in which the circumstances of dying are more important than the unknown transition by death itself. Fear of death is a fear of young people because they are robbed of their futures, fear of the circumstances of dying is the elder's fear. One of the adaptive mechanisms of the young is the future: 'One day I will achieve that'; 'One day I will get around to that.' Thus, confronted with death, the young person may be more upset than an elderly adult. Young profession als and young students feel that *death ought to be* a dominant concern of older adults because the probability of dying goes up with age. Many years ago a great internist, Osler, commented about the fact that in the many deaths he attended, few if any were accompanied by unmanageable fear or anxiety.

I recall that in a study of normal aged persons at the National Institute of Mental Health, it was the young psychiatrists and psychologists who were reluctant to interview the older subjects about death. Concerns of the older person were more with the pragmatics of dying and with the preparation for the transition. It is partly this shift in emphasis which I believe identifies a point about religion in service of the quest of older adults for meaning in their lives, but it may not be resolved by creed or religious formalism.

RELIGION AND HELPING THE AGED

The previous discussion established an important difference between the concerns of the elderly about dying and the concerns of death as a transition. I have made the point that often our professional orientations are generated from the themes of the young. In this instance, the themes are commonly projected onto older adults, just as adult themes are often projected upon children.

In a broader sense, the extent of this projection relates to the fact that America is still a young country in its orientation, and Christianity is a young person's religion. As purely secular commentary, I would offer the view that Jesus and his disciples were young men. Few places in the Old or New Testaments fix responsibility within older persons themselves as to what their obligations are in developing themselves in the later years.

It might be pointed out that in the Japanese, Korean and Chinese societies, the respect for the elderly is demonstrated more highly than it is in America. In the international survey already discussed, it was found that in Japan only 7.8% in the sample surveyed believed in one God. In South Korea 26.4% believed that there is one God. This is in distinction with the United States, where 76.1% professed belief in one God. Thus, reverence for parents does not appear to have a close association with belief in a deity.

I recall a young professor of psychology from South Korea who, in writing his autobiography, identified one of the most significant features about himself as being the fact that he was the eldest son. In China, Korea and Japan, being the eldest son is a most significant role and responsibility, but its strength as an identity, seems to be detached from organized religion.

In his book, *Aging as a Spiritual Journey*, Bianchi suggests that phenomena of aging may be studied from a theological perspective in dealing with matters of spiritual growth and meaning.[1] He discusses the assessment of personal experiences by middle-aged and older persons, fitting the life as it has been led into a larger interpretative whole. We are learning much in these years about biological, psychological, and social aging. How this mass of facts, which is doubling about every 10 years, is interfacing with theology and organized religion is of concern to me. As our society increasingly shows a demographic trend toward more older persons, more commonplace will be the issue of meeting the spiritual quests of old persons. It is very difficult to master the body of literature in one segment of science and aging, let alone as a whole. Yet somehow, our professions must embrace some elements of this literature if they are to serve the older persons of our society in the terms of the older persons and not in the terms of the young. Almost every serious student of adult development and aging has identified a quest in the later years for what might be interpreted as a searching for meaning and organizing metaphors. An individual is expected to have flexibility in these metaphors, and in this twentieth century our secular society is constantly offering new interpretations of the nature of mankind and our relationship to the universe.

One of the characteristics of science is that it can discard, trade-in and trade up its core metaphors from time to time. It is of more than small interest that the comprehensive project on our aging society organized by the Carnegie Corporation did not include an exploration of religion in the comprehensive volume that was published.[8] It would seem that the increasingly secular society of today is depending more and more upon science supplying its root metaphors, rather than the church and theology.

REFERENCE NOTES

1. Eugene Bianchi, *Aging as a Spiritual Journey* (New York: Cross Road, 1984), p. 191.

2. Susan H. McFadden, "Attributes of Religious Maturity in Aging People," *Journal of Religion and Aging* 1 (1985): 39-48.

3. Joseph A. Sittler, "Epilogue: Exploring the Multiple Dimensions of Aging." In, Michael C. Henderickson (Ed.), The Role of the Church in Aging," *Journal of Religion and Aging* 2:1 (1986): 165-172.

4. Michael C. Hendrickson (Ed.), "The Role of the Church in Aging," *Journal of Religion and Aging* 2:1 (1986).

5. Leisure Development Center. "Survey in 13 countries of human values." Presented at the 1980 International Conference on Human Values. (Available from the Secretariat Office, 3-8-1, Kasumigaseki, Chiyoda-ku, Tokyo, 100).

6. Dorcus S. Butt and Morton Beiser, "Successful Aging: A Theme for International Psychology," *Psychology and Aging* 2:1.

7. Bonnie Hedlund, "The Development of Meaning in Life Across Adulthood" (Doctoral Dissertation. Los Angeles: University of Southern California, 1987).

8. Alan Pifer and Lydia Bronte, *Our Aging Society* (New York: Norton, 1986).

Spiritual Development
in the Fourth Quarter of Life

William M. Clements, BD, PhD

SUMMARY. Spirit, the activating or essential principle influencing a person, and body interpenetrate each other but do not dominate each other in predictable ways. Normal aging is neither a failure of the human spirit nor a failure in the body's biology. The spirit becomes more apparent as a result of spiritual development.

The fourth quarter of life covers age 75 to 100 years. Prior to age 75, the human spirit undergoes significant developmental events: a crisis of meaning which may result in conversion or more commonly stripping or shedding; transitions, including loss of clearly defined roles and loss of the sense that the individual's life makes a difference.

One motif applied by our culture to old age is the "iconic illusion"; however, it is evident that in some respects this motif has limited application to the fourth quarter of life. "Meaning making" is, in fact, enhanced in the fourth quarter of life, given reasonable levels of cognitive health. The desire and ability to make sense out of existence, to draw together an understanding of a meaningful life trajectory, is best done in the fourth quarter of life. The dominant sense of time in the fourth quarter of life particularly facilitates spiritual development.

INTRODUCTION

We have become accustomed to looking at the human life cycle in terms of developmental tasks, with certain tasks being especially appropriate for various stages in that cycle. As more and more people in our society become older and older, it is increasingly evident

William M. Clements, PhD, has been appointed Professor of Pastoral Care and Counseling at the School of Theology at Claremont, 1325 N. College Avenue, Claremont, CA 91711.

that the stage of old age has been too comprehensive. There are, at least, the young old and the very old, each, I believe, having appropriate developmental tasks. The very old, including persons in the entire fourth quarter of life, have life experiences and a sense of time that give them a particular opportunity for spiritual growth. The developmental task in this part of the life cycle is, I believe, spiritual development.

I. DEFINITIONS

A. What Is Meant by the Word "Spirit?"

Dictionaries tell us that our English word "spirit" comes from the Latin word *spiritus* — breath. This, in turn, is related to *spirare* — to blow, to breathe. Selectively, my dictionary works at defining spirit in the following fashion: "an animating or vital principle held to give life to physical organisms." The fourth definition is "soul" and is followed by definitions such as "temper or disposition of mind, mental vigor or animation: vivacity." It is seen as: "the immaterial intelligent or sentient part of a person." And finally for our purposes spirit is defined as "the activating or essential principle influencing a person."

1. Body-Spirit Interpenetration

Thus the human spirit is like the breath in that it is seen indirectly and is assumed to be intimately related to the process of breathing, which is concluded from observations of the chest rising and falling in a rhythmical fashion. As our faithful progenitors knew so well, body and spirit are inextricably linked together. What affects your body does interpenetrate your spirit, not totally dominating your spirit, necessarily, but certainly influencing your spirit. Conversely, what affects your spirit can also have significant effects on your body.

The effect of the human spirit on the body is nowhere more dramatically apparent than the widely recognized "placebo" effect found in modern medicine. A placebo effect is not an imaginary improvement in a condition. Real improvement occurs in a real documented condition. The treatment in and of itself cannot account for the improvement. This improvement is called a "placebo" effect. Because patients want to get better, the treatment releases healing mechanisms in a percentage of the patients that otherwise might not have gotten better. Something in their spirit has had some demonstrable effect on their body. How the process works, in fact, remains largely a mystery. However, any idea can be pushed too far and become outrageous.

2. Relationships Between Thoughts and the Body

We seem to have a strong and enduring fascination in America with the notion that our thoughts can routinely change cell biology. I have read many of the books that support this sort of thinking. People feel responsible for "wanting" cancer, or alcoholism, or heart disease, simply because they have the particular affliction, and they assume that having the right thoughts can make it go away.

Since they want it to go away, and it hasn't, then they must either be thinking the wrong thoughts or secretly (and unconsciously, presumably) want the illness. I wish that life was this simple. We could all live to be a thousand years old!

Let's do an experiment. First, let me give you the simple instructions. For the next five minutes, let each of us meditate on changing the color of our eyes. If you have blue eyes, think brown; if you have brown eyes, think blue; and if you have green eyes, think either blue or brown. You must remove any colored contact lenses from your eyes before the experiment, of course. Wish very hard with maximum concentration on the color of eyes you wish to attain. As part of the experiment, each of you must place a bet. You are free to bet on success or failure. If you choose to bet on success in changing the color of your eyes, you may have ten extra minutes to achieve your goal, a 300% increase in the time available to achieve success over the negatively thinking people who bet on failure. Would you bet on success or failure?

Well, I had decided unequivocally to bet on failure—that my thoughts could not change the color of my eyes. It just didn't seem plausible to me that my thoughts could retroactively influence my genetic makeup. Then I remembered hearing the family story that as a child I was known to cry fervently because I had a full head of hair and all the men in my family were bald-headed. Obviously, I wanted to be like every other man in my family. (The author has a shiny bald head.) Well, my wish came true, didn't it! Maybe there is something more to this than I had assumed and I can still change my bet. I do assume, by the way, that no one in the room would bet the family farm on the notion that you can change the color of your eyes simply by means of your thoughts.

Let's do another experiment and get real scientific this time. Let's assume that everyone in the room has an identical cancer. Your form of cancer has invariably proven fatal in the past. (Fortunately, this form of cancer does not exist in actuality since some people have been known to survive just about any disease.) By the way, one out of every three or four of you is going to get cancer anyway, so I don't feel as guilty as I might had I actually given it to all of you. So, now that we all have identical cancers we may proceed with the experiment. Each of you will receive identical state-of-the-art medical care. In addition, because an important breakthrough treatment has just been announced by the National Cancer Institute in Bethesda, Maryland, each of you will be free to participate in a new experimental treatment, or to decline the new treatment and stick to the state-of-the-art treatment. The new experimental treatment consists of taking off all of your clothes and parading in downtown Claremont carrying a sign that reads "Clothes Cause Cancer." The experiment will take place every Friday for a month.

Now, I can predict that some of you will opt out of the experiment and depend on traditional treatment alone. Others of you will try it a time or two. Some hardy fools among us will successfully complete the experiment, having gotten a good suntan in the process. My hypothesis is that the group completing the experiment will live longer than the group declining to participate. Maybe they will only live longer by five minutes on the average, but they will live longer. Would you agree? If the experiment were actually carried out and the suntanned group did, in fact live longer, could we then conclude that walking naked in Claremont with a sign that reads "Clothes Cause Cancer" actually enables a person to live longer with this particular form of cancer? Probably not. We have probably simply selected out of this room those of us who want to live the longest in the worst sort of way. (If you were in the sun-tanned group, you might have lived the longest anyway!)

Our thoughts and meditations do not appear to me to influence genetics, cell structure and things of this nature on a predictable and reproducible schedule. This is not to say that our physical wellness is not influenced by our thoughts and meditations, only that there is probably not a magical connection between what we think and the color of our eyes. Norman Cousins' experience notwithstanding, ideas and desires cannot be depended upon to change physiology day-in and day-out.

What we think, the quality of our relationships with others, our nutrition, our practices in regard to healthy exercise (the list could be considerably extended, of course) do have an important influence on organismic wellness, in terms of our sense of well being, in terms of the prevention of certain illnesses, in terms of helping to create optimal conditions for our bodies to cooperate with nature and medical science for healing to take place, and in terms of coping and adjustment.

Body and spirit interpenetrate each other but do not totally dominate each other in predictable ways. Just as normal aging is not a failure in the body's biology, normal aging is not a failure of the human spirit either.

B. What Is Meant by Development?

Selectively, my dictionary defines "develop" in the following fashion: to evolve the possibilities of; to promote the growth of (as in developing muscles); to make available or usable (as in developing resources); to cause to unfold gradually; to expand by a process of growth; and to become gradually manifest. The overall notion seems to be that you start off with something, and this something evolves, expands or becomes available or usable.

In the case of spiritual development the implication would be that the human spirit evolves and grows, that the spirit becomes more manifest, that it becomes more available and usable. Perhaps it wouldn't be stretching the point too much to assert that the spirit itself becomes more apparent. The spirit is less hidden as a result of spiritual development.

C. What Is Meant by the Fourth Quarter of Life?

The fourth quarter of life begins with the age of 75 and stretches to the 100th year. Thus, all people born before 1915 would be in the fourth quarter of life today. This is a rapidly growing segment of society, obviously. Taken as a whole, the fourth quarter is probably the most rapidly growing age group in America, if you discount sub-groups from within the fourth quarter, such as persons over 80, persons over 90, and so forth. On a more practical level, I have heard it reported that the people at TIAA (Teachers Insurance and Annuity Association) who insure and provide retirement plans for many of our college and university teachers, now expect at retirement that when a married professor retires, one of the couple will survive until the decade of their nineties. The notion of a 25-30 year period of retirement is absolutely unprecedented in world history, of course. As a result of these dramatic demographic shifts, persons in the fourth quarter of life will be of increasing significance in the religious, social, and political arenas in the decades ahead.

II. THE YEARS BEFORE THE FOURTH QUARTER OF LIFE

A. Early Old Age or the Young Old

It is important to keep in mind that some very important things are likely to happen to people on their way to the fourth quarter of their life. The years between 55 and 75 are full of events with developmental implications for the human spirit. Elsewhere I have developed some of these events and themes and have written about their implications. Let me briefly review them for us today.

1. Crisis of Meaning

While I am sure that each age in life may have characteristic spiritual attributes that clearly differentiate it from the others, I would be a bit hard pressed to identify them with any precision.

What does seem more apparent to me, however, is the notion that early old age (that is, the years from 65-75) is the stage of life in which the adequacy of one's previous spirituality is tested mightily by the culture. Early old age is not the quintessential stage for the creation de novo of spiritual maturity.

a. Conversion. From time to time, it undoubtedly happens that a person in old age, who has lived life without concern for inwardly spiritual matters, turns to God and has a conversion experience in which value priorities are reshuffled. Such a conversion enables an individual to move toward a new value orientation that can be embraced and lived out in fullness. However, given a previous life that was more concerned with other matters such as the material, familial, or professional, the radical reshuffling of priorities pointed to by conversion is quite unusual in the seventh and eighth decades of life. While possible, and from my value stance, even desirable, it is the rare exception.

b. Stripping or shedding. What seems to me to be more common, in contrast to conversion as the means of attaining spiritual maturity in the advancing years, is a process that is perhaps even more painful. It does not necessarily lead to a higher spiritual integration; it may, in fact, lead to challenges that are not met. Instead of the repudiation of previously held values that are now rejected because of a conversion, a different process takes place. It has been described as a process of "stripping away."[1] Those cultural and social values learned and practiced in the earlier years are "stripped away" by the same society that had taught them and the same society that had rewarded their attainment in the younger years.

For the person formed by the Christian tradition, this process of "stripping away" can be understood as a sacramental process of "emptying that leads to God."[2] Here "sacramental" is being thought of in terms of the classic definition of "an outward and visible sign of an inward and spiritual grace." As a result of this process, in which the outward and visible sign is one of "stripping away," an emptiness that signifies an inward and spiritual grace can be revealed at the core. Or, an emptiness that is void of sacramental meaning might also be revealed. In either case, the emptiness that has always been present is now revealed in stark nakedness, no longer hidden by the social and cultural props that society has taken away.

But exactly what is stripped away by society? Here I will mention only two concrete examples that help clarify the point.[3] There is an abundance of other examples that, while true, probably only serve to make the same point repeatedly.

B. Transitions in Early Old Age

1. Loss of Clearly Defined Roles

The first example involves the loss of clearly defined roles. In the life span prior to the point of early old age, every age or stage that went before was associated with some measure of social advancement or enhancement. Moving from childhood to adolescence, for example, involves the acquisition of additional freedom (staying up later at night), opportunities (driving an automobile) and responsibilities (holding a part-time job). Each earlier stage, whether that of infancy, childhood, adolescence, or young adulthood, might be thought of as preparation for the following stage. But early old age, at least within the technological and informational culture in which we find ourselves, does not convey the same symbolic advancement or enhancement. Occupational and familial roles can be largely lost or so threatened or modified that they are hardly recognizable.

We are all familiar with the loss of the work-role brought about by the increasing experience of unemployability among late middle-aged people and the same loss from retirement among the "young old." The attendant decrease in income and, perhaps, prestige is already known and described. But what about the loss of clearly defined family relationships that is experienced as a threat to persons from the middle age onward? Consider for a moment the perplexity experienced by the seventy-year-old widow with three married children. The widow remarries and becomes the wife of a man with two adult children of his own from a previous marriage. Her oldest adult child is married and has two married children, each of whom has one child. So far, we can follow fairly well. She is a mother, grandmother, and greatgrandmother in a traditional fashion. The other two of the former widow's adult children are divorced and remarried. One of the remarried adult children is not the custodial parent of his children, who now live with their biological mother. Instead, his second wife has three children from a previous marriage. The second adult child who has remarried is the custodial parent of one child, the biological mother is the custodial parent of another, and his second wife has custody of a child from her previous marriage. If you are not confused yet, just think what you will feel like when I finish with the former widow's new husband, who has his own network of perplexing family relationships.

Now, what is this woman's role as a grandparent? You, along with the seventeen other people in this scenario who might be considered grandparents, would probably experience a considerable measure of role confusion, don't you think? How does the culture (or the church, for that matter) help us along as we sort out our role as grandparent in this situation? Where are the cultural guidelines or templates that can be called upon?

In all of previous life experience there have been extrinsic role expectations from job, family, and friends. With old age, many of these extrinsic role expectations are stripped away by death, retirement, and divorce. Few people seem adequately prepared for the challenges posed by life without the presence of these extrinsic role expectations.

2. Loss of the Sense that My Life Makes a Difference

The second example of what society strips away in old age is the sense that the individual's life, my life, makes a difference. Unfortunately, we are all familiar with the increase in suicide rates among white males in the United States as age advances across the life span. A white male of eighty-five years of age is at greater risk per capita for suicide than a white male of twenty-five or forty-five. This is not true in many of the other societies around the world. We could also consider the rates for alcoholism as important data. Both could point toward a diminution in the sense that "my life makes a difference to someone." We are increasingly living in a service and information society in which the value of "the traditional" has less and less utility in the marketplace of ideas and services. The importance and worth of accumulated wisdom, apart from specific technological knowledge, is largely ignored. Nowhere is this more clearly apparent to me than in modern medicine.

One of my colleagues and friends, who was long "retired," had literally grown up at the feet of Sir William Osler. Sir William Osler is to modern medicine what Adolf Harnack is to Church History or Babe Ruth is to baseball, for those of you unfamiliar with this great pioneer physician-educator. When I learned that my soon-to-be-colleague was joining the faculty as an emeritus member, with an office next door to mine, I was excited. Later, still before his arrival, I recall being concerned about the likely prospect of increased noise from students loitering around waiting to see him. Regardless of disciplines, I have found that students loitering out in the hall make about the same degree of noise as the subway that came out of the tunnel below my window at Union Seminary. Plus, the sound of his door opening and closing incessantly throughout the day would be a major distraction.

As you might have guessed, my concerns were misplaced. Students stayed away in droves from this warm, delightful man who could have imparted so much of value concerning the emergence of modern clinical medicine from the age of leeches and maggots. His "information" was irrelevant to the next exam or to the care of the patient with coronary bypass surgery scheduled for tomorrow. Wisdom and living history have little place in a technological informational service society.

Let me indulge myself in one more example. I was once asked to see a very old man who was quite depressed for no reason that his family, friends, or physicians could determine. He had ample resources and a comfortable home in a beautiful area of the country; he and his wife had been happily married for many years; he had no serious physiological health problems. What was wrong with him? As I sat with him in the late afternoon of his life it seemed to me that he was grieving more than he was depressed. When I tell you that he was a scientist who had spent most of his career in a particular area of research, you may be able to guess. He had been forced into retirement by a mandatory retirement policy perhaps as much as a decade before our meeting, yet his research was still "ongoing." He had even tried to give away his life's work, yet there was no one to take up where he had left off. He felt that all his work would be lost, that his whole professional life had made no difference.

These two losses—clearly defined roles and the sense that "my life makes a difference"—are likely to happen not just to individuals but to an entire group of people, the young old. "Old age is the first stage of life in which people suffer loss because of no personal failures, but simply the attainment of age."[4] If the matter ended here, our collective futures would be pretty bleak. Fortunately, the process of stripping away does not have to represent an end state of existence. Things do not have to end there. In fact, instead of speaking of stripping away it might be less harsh and more accurate to speak of a process like "shedding." Just as a caterpillar sheds its husk to become a butterfly, perhaps the shedding of previous roles and the shedding of the sense that my life makes a difference might be necessary. The process of shedding might be necessary in a developmental sense for the continued spiritual growth of persons in the fourth quarter of life.

III. THE FOURTH QUARTER OF LIFE

A. The Iconic Illusion

Up until this point we have discussed certain changes occurring in the life cycle among the "young old"—persons between 65-75. Now we will turn our attention toward persons in the fourth quarter of life. Certain dominant motifs are used by the culture to explain to itself the human life cycle. One of these motifs has been identified by Paul Pruyser as the "iconic illusion."[5] In this "iconic illusion" development is seen as a series of low-high-low transitions. Life starts out low builds to a peak and then declines.

This motif is clearly seen in physical development, where physical attributes are gained during adolescence, developed in young adulthood, and then decline with the passage of decades. Phil Niekro, the famous knuckle-ball pitcher in professional baseball, is a "phenom" at 44 or so years of age. He has endured more than a decade longer than many of his former colleagues who passed their peak much earlier without a "gimmick" pitch that enabled them to hang on. Or take the family as another example. The typical nuclear family begins with two adults, grows larger, and then declines in number as children grow up and leave home. The problem with the iconic illusion is that it is mistakenly applied to all of life, as if it could explain all of human existence.

1. Limitations to the Iconic Illusion

Many intellectual fields such as that of physics is dominated by the contributions from younger members of the profession. James Van Allen, who discovered the Van Allen Radiation belt around the earth retired recently, having made his famous discovery decades ago, while a young man. Other careers such as in philosophy, theology, and law seem to be tilted toward the later years. In these fields, major creative works are likely to appear in the later years, sometimes significantly after the arbitrary retirement age of 65. Paul Tillich was 77 when his third volume of Systematic Theology was published. Pope John XXIII was considered to be an old, interim pope until he called the second Vatican Council. John Wesley was 81 when he first sent Methodist missionaries to America. The list could go on and on, of course.

The point is that the iconic illusion obscures as much as it illuminates. It obscures that certain capacities do not decline with age and may even increase with advances in age across the life span. These capacities are not subject to a rigid low-high-low sequence of development. Language skills, vocabulary usage and those disciplines closely associated with meaning making, such as law, philosophy and theology develop across the life span.

B. Meaning Making

As a result of these common sense observations, it should be obvious to all that "meaning making" is one capacity that is enhanced in the fourth quarter of life, given reasonable levels of cognitive health. A person's desire and ability to make sense out of their existence, to draw together an understanding of a meaningful life trajectory, is best done in the fourth quarter of life. I assume that for most religious people, meaning making at its core is a spiritual exercise, in which the human spirit relates itself to a wider sweep of history than merely one's personal life trajectory. This

wider sweep of history moves both forward and backward and includes the past and one's hopes for the future.

1. Prolepsis

A second component—one's personal sense of time in the fourth
quarter of life also defies the iconic illusion and contributes to spiritual development. Prolepsis is the assumption of a future act or a
development as if it presently exists or has already been accomplished. For prolepsis even to exist with regard to spiritual development there must exist a hopeful vision of the future that serves as a
growthful lure in the present. We see prolepsis most clearly em-
bodied in the Eucharist. During the Eucharist, we are not merely
looking back and remembering a past event as present reality, we
are also looking forward and anticipating as present reality. The
hope of the eschatological banquet is experienced as a foretaste in
the Eucharist.

a. Personal sense of time. How we utilize and experience the
notion of time is so basic to existence that most of us for most of our
days live without reflecting on or even considering the nature and
meaning of time. The concepts of time that I experience have for
me a visual and an imaginative quality about them that I would like
for you to experience for yourself.

1. Linear time. Visually, imagine yourself standing on a vast,
level plain that stretches before you and behind you farther than
your eye can see. Imagine that you have a gigantic ball of string
beside you that you can roll across the plain, leaving a line of string
from your present position to the point at which you wish to stop. If
you roll the ball in the direction behind you, you go backward in
history. If you roll the ball in front of you, you go forward in time.
Now, it seems to me that our society, with this sort of linear clock
time, believes that the notion of "future" refers only to the distant
future, and that the notion of "history" refers only to the distant
past. As a result of this notion of time, people who become aware of
nearing a finite limit to how far their personal balls of string can be
rolled forward act as if, in the absence of a distant future, there is no
future at all. Experientially, for them there is no future that is worth
pursuing. In such a scheme of meaning the string being unrolled

ahead does not go anywhere. There is no forward movement. There is no vision of future directivity.

2. *Experiential time*. Contrast this linear notion of time with one that is more "present" oriented. Imagine again that you are on the vast plain. This time, instead of a ball of string, you have a Polaroid camera. You turn around and take a picture behind you. As the photo grinds out of the camera, you are surprised to see that it shows you in the act of turning, for this is a very special camera. You catch a glimpse of the photo behind that one and it shows you checking the film in your camera. You turn and look ahead and take a picture. It shows you laying the camera aside, and the one in front of that shows you placing the camera in the case. With this conception of time, the photo that comes out of the camera facing rearward is past time, and the photo that emerges facing forward is future time. Each photo represents a discrete moment of time that is distinguishable from the photo in front, and from the one in back, yet is obviously related to both. My conception is that creativity on the personal level emerges in the gap between your present position and the photo that is nearest to you in front. Creativity, when it comes, does not relate to the distant future. On the personal level the distant future is fantasy. The moment of creative insight, or synthesis, is happening as discrete photos of the near future are being formed so that there is still an opportunity to influence the context of the photo. The creative moment is happening when the future moment exists as possibility, not quite yet reality; when the future moment exists as a glimpse, not a certainty. What you hope to see in that fleeting moment as you catch a glimpse is all important. If you close your eyes, then that action has an influence on your sense of excitement and an influence on your directivity. If you look to the distant future and see nothing, then that action, too, has an influence on the emergence of personal creativity.

3. *The prolepsis of the moment*. The prolepsis of the moment is the moment of spiritual development. Spiritual development is happening in this moment of leaping into the future, or it is not happening at all. What you hope to see influences where you land, or, to continue our image, what sort of photo emerges from your camera of meaning. It takes an act of faith to believe in the not quite yet that enables the vision of growth to emerge into reality.

The content of the proleptic vision will be different for each person. But it is at the point of the proleptic vision that spiritual growth takes place in all ages. Persons in the fourth quarter of life are becoming masters at living in the present moment that merges into the not quite yet. This is the quintessential moment for spiritual development.

In conclusion: It has been asserted that the young old are likely to pass through several crises in the transition to the fourth quarter of life. Two transitions were identified as the loss of roles and the loss of the sense that my life makes a difference. Both of these losses were seen as preparatory for the emergence of a heightened sense of meaning making that is facilitated by the dominant experience of time in the fourth quarter of life. Spiritual development is seen by me as the developmental task for the fourth quarter of life.

NOTES

1. Whitehead, Evelyn Eaton and Whitehead, James D. "Retirement" in *Ministry with the Aging: Designs, Challenges, Foundations*, W. Clements, ed. New York: Harper & Row, Publishers, Inc. 1981, pp. 132-134.
2. Whitehead, Evelyn Eaton, Whitehead, James D.and Meyers, Gordon J., S.J. "The Parish and Sacraments of Adulthood: Accesses to an Educational Future" *Listening: The Journal of Religion and Culture* 12(2)97, 1977.
3. These two points were most recently made by The Rev. Stephen Sapp, Ph.D. in a paper entitled "Views on Aging" delivered at the Seventh Annual Geriatrics Conference on April 17, 1987, at Callaway Gardens in Pine Mountain, Georgia. The conference was sponsored by the Department of Family Practice at The Medical Center, Columbus, Georgia and Martin Army Hospital at Fort Benning, Georgia. For a more complete discussion of these and other points see: Sapp, Stephen, *Full of Years: Aging and the Elderly in the Bible and Today*, Nashville: Abingdon Press, 1987.
4. Op Cit.
5. Pruyser, Paul W. "Aging: Downward, Upward, or Forward?" in *Toward a Theology of Aging*, S. Hiltner, ed., New York, Human Sciences Press, 1975, pp. 102-118.

Factors Which Are Related to Successful Aging in Retired Christian Workers

Jean Albaum, PhD

SUMMARY. The life satisfaction of retired Christian workers was examined to see if the results would support those of research using similar methods but a less unique group of subjects. Data concerning activities, religious beliefs and past traumas were compared to information from the Life Satisfaction Index-A and Constantinople's Inventory of Psychosocial Maturity. The results are not inconsistent with the proposals of continuity theory. However, they indicate that it may be the continuity of activities which continue the ideology, identity or sense of purpose of the individual which are associated with successful aging rather than those which continue patterns of activity for the sake of "activity," per se.

Factors which may be related to successful aging have been the focus of much research during the last thirty years. Early studies were made with large, usually randomly selected, samples of older people.[1,2,3,4,5] The theories of aging which have since dominated the literature were formulated from the results of these early studies.[5,6,7,8] The activity theory proposes that the continuation of the

Jean Albaum is a Life Span Licensed Educational Psychologist and a Marriage, Family, and Child Counselor who has a private practice in Encino, CA. She is associated with a school for orthopedically handicapped students in Claremont, CA and holds a BA in Psychology, a MS in Special Education, a MS in Counseling, and a PhD in Education/Human Development.

This paper was originally prepared for the "Spiritual Maturity and Wholeness in the Later Years" Conference, Claremont, CA, April, 1987.

Address correspondence to the author at 4807 Woodley Avenue, 310; Encino, CA 91436.

level of activities pursued during middle age leads to life satisfaction and successful aging.[4,7,9] The "disengagement" theory proposes that old age is a developmentally different stage from middle age. In this new, final stage of life, successful aging and life satisfaction are achieved through a "mutual withdrawal" which takes place between the individual and society.[6] A third, more currently accepted, "continuity theory" suggests that life satisfaction may be positively related to disengagement for some and to activity for others. Continuity of patterns of individual personality and life style, in terms of activity and social roles, is the primary factor of successful aging.[8,10,11]

In addition, researchers have examined many factors as possible correlates of successful aging. Some of these, such as health and socioeconomic status, have shown strong relationships to life satisfaction in old age. There is evidence that others, such as family relationships and religious beliefs, are also related to the well being of the elderly.[12]

In this study a unique group of retired Christian workers, all of whom were aging successfully, were studied using conventional methods to see if the results would support those of research using similar methods but a less unique group of subjects or whether different results would be obtained specific to the retired Christian workers in this sample. The successful aging of retired Christian workers as a group had never been studied. It was hypothesized that the results of this study would lend support to the proposals of "continuity theory" and that traumatic situations suffered in the past would be associated with less successful aging. Successful aging was defined as "The satisfaction which an individual holds with his or her present and past life" (p.305).[3]

METHOD

Subjects

The subjects of the study were sixty-one American retired Christian workers, all of whom had spent a minimum of three years overseas. Representing ten mainline Protestant denominations, all had given at least twenty years to professional service as ministers, missionaries, Y.M. and Y.W.C.A. directors and teachers of religion. Ten of the subjects described themselves as conservative in religious beliefs and the remainder as liberal. All of the subjects had at least enough income to meet their needs and all lived in independent homes on the grounds of the retirement community. The forty-two women and nineteen men ranged in age from sixty six to ninety six and had been retired from six months to twenty-nine years. All of the women had held paying positions for at least a portion of their lives. The highly unique status of the subjects of this study automatically introduced a number of controls which served to add interesting dimensions to the analysis of the data. All of the subjects ascribed to a religious faith which, among other possible supportive beliefs, assumes a belief in life after death. All of the subjects possessed at least a bachelor's degree, more than two-thirds possessed graduate degrees, and all were well traveled. All lived in a highly ranked retirement community which assured that attractive housing, adequate food and health care needs were met. Unless health or physical restrictions intervened, all had an opportunity to engage in many formal and informal social activities, including eating in central dining halls, if they chose. High status was assigned to residency in the retirement community and the role of "retired Christian worker" was generally well received in the greater surrounding community in which they lived.

Measures

The five dimensions of life satisfaction proposed by Neugarten, Havighurst and Tobin[13] were used to represent the dependent variable, "successful aging." They were measured by the Life Satisfaction Index-A, which incorporates the dimensions of resolution and fortitude, zest, congruence between desired and achieved goals, positive self-concept and mood tone[8] and the Inventory of Psychosocial Maturity.[14] The latter was designed to measure both successful and unsuccessful resolutions of Erik Erikson's first six stages of development. Both instruments have been demonstrated to have satisfactory reliability and validity.[14,15] Each was scored according to the recommendations of the authors.

A total "successful aging" score was computed for each subject by adding the Life Satisfaction Index score and the Inventory of Psychosocial Maturity score. A "total score" test-retest Pearson correlation of .90 was found. This was considered a strong indication of the reliability of the total "successful aging" score. The mean for the subjects (N = 61) was 93.8. The median score was 100.

Possible correlates of successful aging, such as activities of the past and present, the continuity of patterns of activity of the past into the present and traumatic situational conditions of the past were the independent variables. They were measured by the first half of "Your Activities and Attitudes," which was designed by Burgess, Cavan and Havighurst to collect situational and biographical data and to determine levels of activity.[1] In addition, objective and factual questions about the subjects' earlier lives and present religious and travel activities were asked.

The degree of reliability for this measure was shown to be high for use with older populations. It was especially high for factual and attitudinal questions.[16] The instrument has high face validity. Because the objective and factual questions which were added concerning the past were of a nature highly unlikely to be forgotten or misrepresented (such as the death of a parent or sibling), the validity of the additional questions is considered acceptable.

Procedures

The first set of questionnaires mailed to the subjects included the Life Satisfaction Index-A and Constantinople's Psychosocial Maturity Index. A follow up questionnaire consisting of the activities half of "Your Activities and Attitudes" and questions developed for the purposes of this study were mailed six weeks later.

Because the mean on the Life Satisfaction Index for the subjects of this study (15.8) was almost one standard deviation higher than the mean for the subjects of the Neugarten, Havighurst and Tobin[8] sample (12.4, S.D. = 4.4), the subjects of this study were divided into two groups considered average and high "successful agers." The "successful aging" total score was used as the representation of the dependent variable "successful aging." The groups were divided at the median (100) of the total "successful aging" score (high n = 30, average n = 31). The median was used instead of the mean (93.8) because of the small sample size.

RESULTS

The data were analyzed in a search for associations between "successful aging," as measured by the successful aging total score, and activities of the past and present, the continuity of patterns of activity of the past into the present, and traumatic situational conditions of the past.

Although the total number of activities ranged from two to more than twenty-five, no associations of any kind were found between the number of activities of this group of subjects and successful aging. This was true of both present and past activities (Table 1). The only significant relationship which was found between the continuation of the patterns of activity of the past into the present and successful aging suggested that those individuals who saw their families more now than at mid-life were more likely to be in the average than the high group (Table 2).

The subjects who had lost a sibling during childhood were more likely to be in the average than the high group of "successful agers" (Table 3). Significant associations were found between feeling very satisfied about accomplishments and feeling that one's overall life had been happy and successful aging (Table 4).

It was found that in spite of a wide range in the nature, as well as the number of most of their activities, virtually all of the subjects were highly active and involved in areas of religion. Close to ninety-seven percent of all of the subjects attended religious services four to ten times per month. Only one attended less. Sixty-seven percent engaged in some form of daily religious activity in their homes. Seventy-eight percent attended religious services the same to more than they had in mid-life.

Many additional, personal comments about religion were added spontaneously. For example, in discussing death, only one expressed any fear. In discussing how they viewed their ideology and spirituality with relationship to aging, many offered moving descriptions of the continued opportunity for growth and development which this stage of life provided. They wrote of time for meditation

Table 1

Activities of the Past and Present

Compared to Successful Aging Total

Activities	t Statistic	df's	χ^2	df's
How often see family now	.16	59		
Number of confidential friends	-1.03	33		
Regular leisure activities	.16	59		
A trip is planned	.88	59		
Religious services monthly	.00	59		
Home religious activity	- .52	59		
Total present religious activity	- .52	59		
Religious services before retirement	- .68	58		
Taking care of home			.294	3
Total friends, leisure, religious and paid activities now	- .70	44		
Happy with present activities			2.73	3
Leisure activities before retirement	- .05	59		

and reflection, of changing broadening values and of finding joy in the "commonplace."

DISCUSSION

Some interesting questions were raised by the almost complete absence of any associations between successful aging and the activity levels of this group of subjects.

The "life-satisfaction" literature presents fairly conclusive evidence that a relationship exists between activity levels and successful aging. In addition, the concept that the continuity of activity levels of the past into the present has a relationship to successful

Table 2

Continuation of Pattern of Activities of the Past into
the Present Compared with Successful Aging Total

Activities	t Statistic	df's	χ^2	df's
See family more or less now			6.03*	2
See friends more or less now			.352	2
Attend religious services more or less now			.283	2
More or less organizations now			.565	2
More or less leisure activity now			.460	2
Change in number of activities	-.86	59		
Total friends, organizations and religious services, more or less now	.54	59		
Continue vocation into retirement			.711	1

*Significant at the .05 level.

aging has been consistently supported.[12] However, neither relationship was found for this highly unique group of individuals in spite
of the fact that the number of activities ranged from two to more
than twenty-five. In the search for possible explanations of these
results the nature of the activities which the subjects pursued was
examined.

Whether their overall level of activity was high, medium or low,
all of the subjects engaged in activity which continued a major central theme of their lives. Current religious beliefs and activities were
consistent with self-reported childhood and mid-life beliefs and activities. Religious beliefs, and the activities that resulted from them,
provided the subjects with their professions, their identities and a
lifelong sense of purpose. Carried into retirement they continued to
provide identities and a sense of purpose for the subjects. The situation in which activities which were continued from the past included at least some which focused around an ongoing central

Table 3

Traumatic Situational Conditions of the Past and Present

Compared with Successful Aging Total

Trauma	t Statistic	df's	n's	% Age of Total
Sibling died during subject's childhood	2.75**	59	15	24.6
Father died during subject's childhood	- .06	59	10	16.4
Mother died during subject's childhood	- .50	59	5	8.2
Suffered childhood illness longer than three months	-1.25	59	7	11.5
Suffered midlife illness longer than six months	- .50	59	5	8.2
Spouse died in subject's early or midlife	- .05	59	8	13.1
Children died in subject's early or midlife	- .74	59	10	16.4
First hand experience of war	.68	59	23	37.7
Loss of wealth or possessions	1.07	58	14	23.0
Loss changed life style	- .94	58	6	9.8
Life's work destroyed	.53	58	3	4.9
Other early traumas	.85	59	34	55.6
Death of spouse since retirement	.43	59	12	19.7
Death of child since subject's retirement	- .54	58	5	8.2
Death of siblings since subject's retirement	-1.20	58	17	27.8
Other traumas since retirement	- .50	59	5	8.2
Total trauma score	.56	59		

**Significant at the .01 level.

Table 4

Accomplishments and Successes Compared

with Successful Aging Total

Accomplishments and Successes	t Statistic	df's	χ^2	df's	Pearson r	p
Honors	- .95	59				
Happiness of last marriage			1.54	3		
Success of children			2.72	3		
Consider life happy			3.72*	1		
Feel about accomplishments					.51	.000***
Total accomplishments	-1.88	59				

*Significant at the .05 level.

***Significant at the .000 level.

theme was not necessarily true for the subjects of other studies. The explanation for the unusual results found with this unusual group of subjects may lie in this area.

The possibility arises that it may not be the number of activities or the continuation of a pattern of amounts of activity from the past into the present which is the most important factor associated with successful aging. Instead, it may be the contribution which those activities and patterns which are carried into old age, whatever their number, make to the continuing identity, ideology and sense of purpose of the individual. If the important aspect of the activities was the nature of the activities rather than the number, and the nature of the important activities for the subjects of this study was shared by all, then it would follow that the different degrees of life satisfaction experienced by the subjects would arise out of aspects of their lives other than their activities, as was the case for these subjects.

Although the results of this study found little support for the tenets of activity theory, they are not inconsistent with the proposals of continuity theory. However, the emphasis is different. The results of this study indicate that it may be the continuity of activities which continue the ideology, identity or sense of purpose of the individual which are associated with successful aging rather than the continuity of activities which simply continue patterns of activity for the sake of "activity," per se.

The relationship which was found between the death of a sibling during childhood and successful aging was highly interesting. Although the sample of subjects who had lost siblings during their childhoods was small (n = 15), the relationship was significant at the .01 level. If this relationship could also be found in larger studies, it could have important implications for parents, religious workers, mental health professionals and doctors who work with the families of children who have died.

The association in this study between seeing one's family more than once a week and lower successful aging was similar to an association found by Kutner et al.[4] with a large sample of aging subjects. It, too, could have implications for religious workers and mental health professionals who work with aging individuals and their families.

This unique group of subjects in a highly favorable position introduced a number of controls into the study. Probably because of this, no low "successful aging" group was found. The differences between the average and high groups were slightly, but far from fully, explained by the results of this study. The factors which may be associated with average versus high levels of successful aging for this sample may not be those frequently studied by researchers. The reasons may well be found among subtle, perhaps internal, variables such as psychological and/or spiritual differences which could not be measured effectively by the methods used in this study. In addition, because of the limited nature of the sample, generalization of the results of this study to other populations must be done with caution.

NOTES

1. Burgess, E., R. Cavan, and R. Havighurst. 1948. *Your activities and attitudes*. Chicago: Science Research Associates.

2. Dell Lebo, L. 1953. Some factors said to make for happiness in old age. *Journal of Clinical Psychology* 9:385-390.

3. Havighurst, R. 1963. Successful aging. In R. Williams, C. Tibbits, and W. Donahue, eds., *Processes of aging*. New York: Atherton Press.

4. Kutner, B., D. Fanshel, A. Togo, and T. Langner. 1956. *Five hundred over sixty*. New York: Russell Sage Foundation.

5. Maddox, G. 1968. Persistence of life style among the elderly: A longitudinal study of patterns of social activity in relation to life satisfaction. In B. N. Neugarten, ed., *Middle age and aging*. Chicago: University of Chicago Press.

6. Cumming, E., and W. Henry. 1961. *Growing old: The process of disengagement*. New York: Basic Books, Inc.

7. Havighurst, R., B. Neugarten, and S. Tobin. 1968. Disengagement and patterns of aging. In B. N. Neugarten, ed., *Middle age and aging*. Chicago: University of Chicago Press.

8. Neugarten, B., R. Havighurst, and S. Tobin. 1968. Disengagement and patterns of aging. In B. N. Neugarten, ed., *Middle age and aging*. Chicago: University of Chicago Press.

9. Havighurst, R., and R. Albrecht. 1953. *Older people*. New York: Longmans Green.

10. Reichard, S., F. Livson, and G. Peterson. 1968. Adjustment to retirement. In B. N. Neugarten, ed., *Middle age and aging*. Chicago: University of Chicago Press.

11. Rose, A. 1968. A current theoretical issue in social gerontology. In B. N. Neugarten, ed., *Middle age and aging*. Chicago: University of Chicago Press.

12. Larson, R. 1978. Thirty years of research on the subjective well-being of older Americans. *Journal of Gerontology* 33:109-125.

13. Neugarten, B., R. Havighurst, and S. Tobin. 1961. The measurement of life satisfaction. *Journal of Gerontology* 16:134-143.

14. Constantinople, A. 1969. An Eriksonian measure of personality development in college students. *Developmental Psychology* 1:357-372.

15. Wood, V., M. Wylie, and B. Sheafor. 1969. An analysis of a short self-report measure of life satisfaction: Correlation with rater judgments. *Journal of Gerontology* 24:464-469.

16. Cavan, R., E. Burgess, R. Havighurst, and H. Goldhammer. 1949. *Personal adjustment in old age*. Chicago: Science Research Associates.

Spiritual Dimension
of Human Sexuality

Calvin Ammerman, ThD

SUMMARY. The quest for spiritual maturity may be likened to a spiritual odyssey. This paper represents research concerning the spiritual dimension of human sexuality. Diminishment and loss are givens of the senior years. Loss is exacerbated in relationships defined by fidelity and commitment.

Four headings outline the paper; an extensive bibliography supports and documents the essays. *End to Innocence*: we are next. Common parlance dwells on myths of aging, while there are distinct realities of aged sexuality. Loneliness can be devastating; there must be more creative societal responses to the human condition of old and alone. *Love Revisited*: read, sexual desire and love. Historical perspective re-examines *eros* and *agape*; literature, which is bigger than life, is a much neglected resource — and an illuminating one. When confronting mystery, the poet and novelist may provide the language we need to comprehend the phenomenon of love (and grace). *Human Sexuality and Spirituality*: Hebrew-Christian and Eastern religions (Taoism and Tantric Sex) have somewhat to say in terms of sexuality and spiritual pilgrimage. *Acquiescence*: human values of touching, intimacy, friendship, and vulnerability must be considered.

> Old age hath yet his honor and his toil;
> Death closes all: but something ere the end,
> Some work of noble note, may yet be done,
> Not unbecoming men that strove with Gods.[1]

Somehow, Tennyson captures the essence of aging and of spiritual odyssey in this fragment. Were we to read "Ulysses" in its entirety, we would discover an idle king who had always roamed

---

Calvin Ammerman is affiliated with the Augustana Lutheran Church, 5000 East Alameda Avenue, Denver, CO 80222.

with hungry heart now confined to a hearth with an aged wife. The perceptive reader will intuit a sexual residual and its spiritual linkage.

I. END TO INNOCENCE

A major life goal should be to face ultimate realities with an equanimity tempered by the years. No one has promised that such an adventure in living would be particularly easy. As Sheldon Kopp comes down to the wire, admitting that he is scared and uncertain in the face of terminal illness, he recognizes that his original innocence has been compromised and surrendered.[2] His book title is appropriated without disservice. Soon or late, we must face the realities of the present situation stripped bare of unrealistic expectations.

We are next. . . . On closer inspection, this simple sentence is truly ominous. Alex Comfort's primary claim to fame resides between the covers of *The Joy of Sex*, but he is also to be credited with the simple but elegantly complicated truth which is so difficult to accept: "We are next."[3] No good answer is forthcoming as to why it is so exquisitely painful for us to confront our mortality, but when that threshold is crossed, the work of aging has begun.

Just because we finally come to terms with aging does not indicate that we cease to have basic human needs that seek fulfillment. We live in a culture which places a premium on youthfulness, and aging is denigrated. Rubin's *Sexual Life After Sixty* stresses that the denial of libidinous feelings is as dangerous in old age as in youth. "Today, there is no longer any reason for anyone to continue to believe that sex, love, and marriage — and romance — are the exclusive privilege of youth."[4]

Trends and projections are laced with facts and figures. When James Peterson wrote his *Married Love in the Middle Years*, old age was determined to have been 70-plus, and he observed that the average male could extend his sexual life by cultivating desire and good health practices.[5] *Aging America* was issued by the United States Department of Health and Human Services (1985-86). This document projects more than twelve million Americans between the ages of 75 and 84 in the year 2000. The 85-plus population (the very old) is expected to increase seven times by year 2050. Sexual demographics translates into ten elderly women to four elderly men — a disparity based on life-expectancy.[6]

In terms of male sexuality, Esquire's publication, *How a Man Ages*, includes a chapter on maintenance which promises much and delivers less, briefing readers on what is already known, innately, that aging brings a cessation of "ejaculatory inevitability" and an increased refractory period between sexual expressions.[7] Add to this the unpleasant prospect that almost every male may anticipate an enlarged prostate gland for having outwitted time.

Doubtless, the very best statement on the realities of human sexuality is to be found in Simone de Beauvoir's *The Coming of Age*. Her long association/relationship with Jean Paul Sartre equipped her to write both eloquently and pointedly concerning male sexuality as well as female sexuality:

> It is true that normally desire does not arise as mere desire — as desire in itself: it is desire for a particular pleasure or a particular body. But when it no longer arises spontaneously, reflection may very well regret its disappearance. The old person often desires to desire because he retains his longing for experiences that can never be replaced and because he is still attached to the erotic world he built up in his youth or maturity — desire will enable him to renew its fading colours. And again it is by means of desire that he will have an awareness of his own integrity. We wish for eternal youth, and this youth implies the survival of the libido.[8]

Simone de Beauvoir places a positive value on sexuality while noting public opinion which the individual tends to accept in terms of propriety and continence. Embarrassment and denial of desires may be thrown back into the unconscious mind. The loss of a long-standing partner may result in traumatization capable of shutting down all sexual activities.[9]

The sexual fabric of many families is so fragile that it is quite unable to countenance the sexual needs of an aging member of the family. A 102-year-old man was interviewed by a reporter from *Modern Maturity*. His children, grandchildren, and great grandchildren informed him that he should act his age (whatever that may have meant).[10] On slightly less grand scale but more pre-eminent, Will and Ariel Durant *(Story of Civilization* authors) had been married 68 years when they died in 1981. An autobiography prints a love poem dated Christmas 1912 which the fiery Canadian Catholic had penned to his Jewish child-bride. The sexual testament was given by Will when he was 85 after 57 years of marriage:

> My modest fires cooled after seventy, and have now reluctantly died out in this year 1970 — so that this book ends fitly.[11]

II. LOVE REVISITED

The classic work on *Agape* and *Eros* is by Anders Nygren. Published first in Great Britain in 1932, he walks us through Plato's writings, asking us to avoid the tendency to equate *Eros* with sensual, earthly love and *Agape* with heavenly, spiritual love.[12] Certainly, there is passion in *Eros*, for the chief characteristics are human desire, a will to possess, and acquisition, but Plato's *Symposium* presents a *Divine Eros* — an ennobling love which is directed upwards ultimately toward a World of Ideas. "God's love, which determines the character of fellowship with God is the archetype of all that can be called Agape."[13] Stated otherwise, *Eros* is "self-love" and *Agape* is "God's love."

Many other designations have been given contrasting and describing love and sexual desire. Martin Luther's *Heidelberg Disputation* of 1518 calls Latin into service instead of Greek: *Amor Dei* and *Amor hominus*; the distinction made was that the love of God is creative, and the love of man is acquisitive.[14] In passing, it should be noted that Luther left the Augustinian order, married a former nun, and sired a passel of children. He was an earthy, sensual, and sexual person — a man of passion as well as a man of God. When John Welwood writes of love, sex, and intimacy, he pairs conditional and unconditional love, both of which serve to delineate human beings. He pinpoints unconditional love most vividly in beginnings and endings — birth and death.[15] Alan Watts devotes a chapter to Sacred and Profane Love.[16] Norman Pittenger refers to the "ecstacy of love" and the "anguish of love," alluding to folk wisdom which understands by experience that love makes demands, requires sacrifice, and causes suffering.[17] But surely, the most original statement of all is to be found in Robert Johnson's chapter, "Stirring the Oatmeal."[18] By this brilliant symbol, he brings love down to the ordinary and the totally unromantic plane — but no less spiritual. Somewhere between earning a living and taking out the garbage, sexual love tends to make or break a marriage.

Denis de Rougemont and Morton Hunt provide our best assessments of romantic love in the Western World. They move us into European literature and explore the romance of Tristan and Iseult, a myth of adultery, which is the very essence of tragedy.[19] The courtly love which grew up out of this pagan love affair with life so idealized woman that sexual intercourse could be postponed indefinitely in some wild infatuation with wholly subjective feelings. As de Rougemont describes vaulted romantic love, it becomes clear that love is being in love with love!

Two very dissimilar love stories deserve attention. Leslie Fiedler, literary critic, cites Dante's "Stony Sestina." This is a poem *about* love. The literary pattern is complicated and is controlled by a mathematical formula. Six short stanzas exhaust the possibilities, and six key words summarize. Interesting but unimportant. What is important is the scenario: an old man in a frozen world confronts a beautiful young girl who is immune to passion — unmoved as a stone. The old man is a portrait of abject despair. Three lines (translated by Fiedler) suffice to tell his bitter tale:

> Whatever time the hills cast blackest shade,
> Beneath a lovely green, my little queen
> Annuls it, as a stone is drowned in grass.[20]

An entirely different love scene is depicted in Par Lagerkvist's short story, *The Marriage Feast*. This describes a home wedding of Frida Johansson and Jonas Samuelsson, elderly Swedish lovers. A few guests come together to celebrate a proper wedding. Two people are made *One* before God. Neither had been married previously. At this time in life, they determined to overcome their loneliness. She wasn't beautiful; he wasn't handsome. Mainly, he loved her because she "bothered" to love him. While guests were imbibing in the kitchen, the happy pair retired to "their" bedroom on the second floor, undressed, and made love for the very first time. Yes, the first time. Theirs was a sacred feeling; neither would be lonely any more. "Their souls were drawn to each other, reach out to each other in ardent longing, call to each other like twittering birds, like animals in their stalls in the evening."[21]

The parting word on sexual desire comes from the poet's poet, Rainer Maria Rilke: "Sex is difficult; yes."[22] He elaborates on that theme as he interprets his own poem, "Requiem." Love is the most difficult task imposed on human beings; it is the work for which all other work is but a preparation.[23]

III. HUMAN SEXUALITY AND SPIRITUALITY

> An aged man is but a paltry thing.
> A tattered coat upon a stick, unless
> Soul clap its hands and sing . . .[24]

That quotation from "Sailing to Byzantium" is William Butler Yeats' way of linking aging and spiritual journey, and Eugene Bianchi includes it in his meaningful monograph of the same title.

There is something about sex that frightens and embarrasses. Relious writers tend to sanitize the text and soar euphorically. Euphemisms pervade. Golden opportunities are evaded by linking, almost exclusively, spirituality to prayer, worship, and Christian service. This is done as Charles Shelton treats *Adolescent Spirituality*.[25] More to the point is John Moore's *Sexuality* and *Spirituality* which he introduces by narrating a visit to a monastery in Scotland where the vacant stares of the ascetics provoked the author to ask himself if any of these noble gentlemen had ever experienced sex with a woman. He turned to the Southern Hemisphere and found himself with naked Indians in Brazil. Protocol prompted him to shed his clothes, and the stage was set to pry spirituality from the strictures of formal religious practice.[26]

Very briefly, Hebrew-Christian and Eastern religion must be assayed in terms of sexuality and spiritual pilgrimage. The clearest and most ordered statement found of the Hebraic-Christian's position on human sexuality is in Eric Fuchs' *Sexual Desire and Love*. The book is summarized in a set of theses (at least ninety) which reflect careful scholarship and penetrating analysis. A few are restated, trusting the essence is fairly presented.

Sexuality is the domain of rules. Unlike animals, the life force in humans cannot be regulated naturally. The potential for violence is always present. Historically, meaning has been ascribed to sexuality by making it sacred. Acknowledging that sexuality participated in the creative work of God, marks the beginning of a theological approach to sexuality; sexuality is thereby established as a gift from God. Sin enters human experience in a garden setting, and a sense of shame caused humankind to cover its nakedness. The priestly Hebraic tradition set forth manifold regulations governing cleanness and uncleanness in Levitical code. Marriage is deemed a gift of God, and the Song of Solomon survived to extol the wonders of conjugal love. Jesus rescued marriage from natural necessity, gave it a value, and by example allowed celibacy to become a vocation. The Apostle Paul's teaching on marriage and individual rights must be seen from an eschatological perspective. For the first 200 years of Christianity, the Christian ideal for marriage was fidelity and chastity with due respect for the most vulnerable in society — slaves, children, and women. Christian theologians (primarily Irenaeus and Tertullian) began to advance an exaggerated asceticism which disfavored sex and marriage. With the moral theology of Augustine, sexuality was directly linked to sin, and a dualism of good/evil and spirit/body (while Manichaean) became a Christian postulate. Virginity was declared to be superior to marriage and sex was countenanced as a means of procreation. By the high Middle Ages, the doctrine of Original Sin (sin transmitted via sexuality) was well-established. Thomas Aquinas applied sacramental grace to conjugal love. The Protestant Reformers rejected the ecclesiastical requirement of celibacy and the concept of marriage as a sacrament.[27] That one extended paragraph covers several thousand years of human history, and Fuchs concludes his statement with two memorable paragraphs.

> Sexual pleasure leads man and woman to a consciousness of the profundity of their existence, which belongs to the spiritual order. In the experience of love, which is both the encounter

of bodies and the approach of the mystery of persons when bodily union does not change, man and woman can discover that the spirit is not truly received until the bodily flesh of existence is not denied but celebrated. The other is both the body close at hand and the irreducible mystery of a presence. Thus man and woman can celebrate, through the fragile language of their bodies, the mystery of the world and of God.

An authentic spirituality of vulnerability and of gift can therefore undergird the erotic celebration of love. . . . The body of the other is a sign that must be deciphered, a hope to be perceived, a gift to be accepted, a presence to be welcomed.[28]

It goes without saying that such noble sentiments are far from the minds and bodies of rank and file lovers—young or old, but someone needs to make a statement concerning human sexuality at its finest level (spiritual). Pittenger reminds us of a Latin phrase from an ancient liturgy which reads: *"ubi amor et caritas, ibi Deus est."* Loosely translated, "Where love and grace are present, there God is working."[29]

When we turn our glance to Eastern religion, the canvas is so immense that almost anything is possible. As Moore discusses sexuality and spirituality, he gives a Vedic interpretation. The two words (sexuality and spirituality) represent two aspects of total energy-flow experienced by the human being. Sexuality is the desire for pleasure, information, and longevity; spirituality is the desire for lasting happiness, true knowledge, and immortality.[30] Alan Watts finds a widely prevalent conflict between spirituality and sexuality in both Western and Eastern religions: abstinence and freedom from lust are prerequisites for spiritual development.[31] While this might be challenged, both Taoist and Tantric sex do place a certain premium on discipline, control, and semen retention during sexual activity. We have already traced Hebraic/Christian sexual thought which might have included reference to "spiritual marriage" that flourished in Alexandria during the second and third centuries A.D. Pairs took vows of celibacy following the marriage and lived as brothers and sisters given over to contemplation and adoration of God.[32]

Taoism is more of a philosophy than a religion. The ancient Chinese refined methods of increasing sexual vitality. Their goal seemed to be the integration of divine and subtle energies into the human body by achieving a balance of the opposing energies (masculine and feminine) called *yin* and *yang*. Esoteric yoga is neither a religion nor a way of salvation; harmony may be the equivalent of the Western concept of love. There is an effort to quiet the ego, calm the mind, and cultivate energy.[33] Western sexologists and mainline Protestant Christianity reject and dismiss most of this, but the lure of spiritual enlightenment and the practice of yoga therapy are not easily retired. The history is long and rich, and it has now become entrenched in holistic health. The principles behind Taoism and Tantra are nearly identical, though Taoism is considered to be the older. Life (sexual) experience is the starting point for spiritual growth, and the goal is Truth. *Telesis*.

Both Taoism and Tantra by philosophy and practice present sexuality as sacramental. Sacramentalism has been in and out of Christian theology. Marriage has been both accorded and denied standing as a sacrament. As Ohanneson writes of sexuality as prophecy, sexuality is likened to mystery which pervades all of human life; in that life is sacred, sexuality which strives for intimacy becomes sacramental.[34] That is not difficult to accept if we refuse to divide life into sacred and profane. Indeed, nothing is more sacred or valued than our sexuality. And the sacramental is an opportunity for growth — growth in love. It may take years of loving, agonizing, reconciling, reconstituting before the gravity of a relationship is truly recognized. In the realignment, sexuality almost becomes spirituality as love transforms and the deeper realities of life are experienced.

The aged and nearly blind ethicist, Joseph Sittler articulates the human dilemma: "And the word *spirituality* — the power, presence, dynamics of the spirit — is not a definable reality." While he is not thinking in terms of sexuality, in a generic sense he *is* as he counsels, "Each person's pilgrimage into a profounder spirituality is a highly personal matter." Sittler is referencing the whole nature of man/woman.[35]

IV. ACQUIESCENCE

Ah, but what can we take along
into that other realm? Not the art of looking,
which is learned so slowly, and nothing that happened

> here. Nothing. The sufferings, then. And, above all,
> the heaviness, and the long experience of love, —
> just what is unsayable.[36]

Marvelous! First, *spirituality* becomes undefinable; then, the long experience of *love* is declared unsayable. However, Rilke, better than anyone else, looks at life and pens what really needs to be said concerning love and death. Acquiescence is quiet, tacit acceptance of that which cannot be changed. It serves no worthwhile purpose to rail against the ravages of aging, to recite a tired set of myths about chronological aging vs. functional aging. Denial of reality seems totally unbecoming intelligent, well-informed leaders. In some respects, if we view aging sexuality as a problem, then we have a human condition without a solution. Old age is a time of diminishment. Sittler deserves to speak again. Lucid and nearing ninety, his *last* book states: "The demand is, rather, for courage, acquiescence, resignation, acceptance—some coming to terms with."[37] And just at this point, James Nelson's definitions of spirituality and sexuality are both fitting and appropriate:

> By *spirituality* I mean not only the conscious religious disciplines and practices through which human beings relate to God, but more inclusively the whole style and meaning of our relationship to that which we perceive as of ultimate worth and power. . . . *Sexuality* is our way of being in the world as female or male persons. . . . In sum, sexuality always involves much more than what we do with our genitals. More fundamentally, it is who we are as body-selves who experience the emotional, cognitive, physical, and spiritual need for intimate communion, both creaturely and divine.[38]

A certain and deliberate acquiescence must be made to aging sexuality. We can "rage against the dying of the light" in Dylan Thomas style, or we can go about our business of "gathering up and sorting out, discriminating between the abiding and the evanescent" in Sittler fashion.[39] As Erickson analyzes the final stage of life, he finds the theme of the last crisis to be *integrity* vs. *despair*.[40]

To be sure, there is an acquiescence akin to silliness. We can acknowledge all sorts of nonsense; we can become condescending and deferential without cause. Respect drains out of relationships, and a mutual toleration (unkind and desperate) marks many elderly relationships. We are caused to wonder: did love ever characterize this union? The apocryphal book, *Ecclesiasticus*, names three sights which warm the heart and three which arouse hatred: "concord among brother, friendship among neighbours, and a man and wife who are inseparable — a poor man who boasts, a rich man who lies, and an old fool who commits adultery."[41] Acquiescence to the fact of aging sexuality might spare us a lot of misery and unhappiness. Declining sexual vigor, dissatisfaction with an aging sexual partner, and temporary impotence have occasioned unfaithfulness many times over. Lest it be assumed that the only thing considered is a heterosexual and monogamous relationship properly sanctioned and atoned by the church, *relationship* is the word to remember. There are a lot of unmarried lovers in our world — many among the senior communities who, for one reason or another, do not choose to marry. Among younger and more urbane citizens, Bob Shacochis gives this rationale:

> We observed our friends marry and divorce, remarry and divorce again. Sacred vows of matrimony, eh? We weren't selling stock to the public; we didn't need a church to instruct us about what we already knew: that we were blessed, bonded, and under obligation not to destroy each other, as seemed to be the current style.[42]

An ethical principle has just been stated: an obligation not to destroy each other. In extreme old age when the ejaculation is no longer vigorous, when the semen barely seeps out, and the vaginal walls are thin and with inadequate lubrication, something yet is required which can be delivered. And that is *touching*. Matthew Fox advocates "sensual spirituality." That means to participate in life's mysteries — to touch, caress, forgive, look at rainbows, hear the waves lapping, smell the lilacs, and taste the wine.[43] Henri Nouwen advocates intimacy, fecundity, and ecstasy; he found this trio in a house of love — a house of friendship among the handicapped in Trosly-Breuil, France. Home! "Home is where we can laugh and cry, embrace and dance, sleep long and dream quietly, eat, read, play, watch the fire, listen to music, and be with a friend.''[44]

Acquiescence must come to terms with separation and loss — and some of that pain has to do with past loves and a lover who is no longer there to offer compassion and care and tenderness. Ashley Montague reminds us that not only the child but the adult needs tender loving care, and that some women entice men into sex relations when all they really want is to be held — to be touched.[45]

Hugh Prather discusses growing old together, noting that the lifelong companion is well aware of the toll that aging is taking — cannot be fooled — "hair is thinning, the breasts are sagging, the stomach dropping, the memory slipping, the sexual organs becoming unarousable, the digestion demanding an ever higher price for indulgence." Still, he cautions that this is the time to cherish the partner: "Bless every white hair, every degree of stoop, every line, every blemish and bruise. This person truly loves you, and the vessel that contains love is sacred."[46] But together or apart, when the fires of passion have cooled or gone out, the moments of greatest happiness and satisfaction will doubtless derive from sexual experience in the handing on of the torch of life. While there may be ambivalence, even hostility with adult children, chances are, grandchildren are sources of almost undiluted joy.

Extreme old age is but a pale reflection of the strength and vitality of youth and a remembrance of things past. There is something almost redemptive about laughter, especially when you are able to laugh at yourself. George Burns has this gift. On the celebrated occasion of his ninetieth birthday as he danced and puffed away on his ever-present cigar, a television audience of millions heard him jest about sex being just a memory. True or not, George is a shining example of vitality and creativity.

So, we are next — aging is unavoidable; love has been revisited; aging human sexuality and spirituality have been considered; and in a conclusion where nothing much has been concluded, the appeal has been to acquiesce — to accept the realities of growing old. The most vulnerable among us still need intimacy, touching, and friendship. The paper began and ends with poetry:

I see your sisters angry, embittered, whining, complaining,
Distressed at life's ending, resenting their children,
While somehow you have outwitted death by living,
Somehow moved beyond time and tragedy to wonder,
Until all your wrinkles lead to your eyes and disappear
In some soft and mysterious immortality.[47]

NOTES

1. Tennyson, Alfred Lord (1842). "Ulysses," *The Poetical Works*. New York: George Routledge and Sons, p. 56.

2. Kopp, Sheldon (1981). *An End to Innocence*. New York: Macmillan Bantam Books, p. 166.

3. Gross, Ronald, Beatrice Gross, Sylvia Seidman (1987). *The New Old*. Garden City: Doubleday, Anchor Press, i.

4. Rubin, Isadore (1965). *Sexual Life After Sixty*. New York: Basic Books, p. 12.

5. Peterson, James. (1968). *Married Love in the Middle Years*. New York: Association Press, p. 81.

6. *Aging America* (1985-1986). Washington, D.C. U.S. Department of Health and Human Services, pp. 1-12.

7. Pesman, Curtis (1984). *How a Man Ages*. New York: Esquire Press, pp. 95ff.

8. de Beauvoir, Simone (1973). *The Coming of Age*, translated by Patrick O'Brian. New York: Warner Books, p. 474.

9. *Ibid.*, p. 477.

10. *Modern Maturity* (April/May, 1986). "Man Bites Doggone Reporter," William Manners. Lakewood, Ca.: A. A. R. P., p. WC7.

11. Durant, Will and Ariel Durant (1977). *A Dual Autobiography*. New York: Simon and Schuster, p. 402.

12. Nygren, Anders (1953). *Agape and Eros*. Published first in Great Britain, 1932. Translation by Philip Watson. Philadelphia: Westminster Press, pp. 50, 176.

13. *Ibid.*, p. 126.

14. *Ibid.* Nygren citing Martin Luther's "Heidelberg Disputation," from Complete Works of Luther, Vol. 30, p. 725.

15. Welwood, John (Ed.) (1985). *Challenge of the Heart*, ch. "On Love: conditional and unconditional" by Welwood. Boston: Shambhala, pp. 60ff.

16. Watts, Alan (1958). *Nature, Man, and Woman*, ch. 7, "Sacred and Profane Love." New York: Pantheon, 1958, pp. 166ff.

17. Pittenger, W. Norman (1974). *Love and Control in Sexuality*. Philadelphia: United Church Press, p. 67.

18. Welwood, John (Ed.) (1985). "Stirring the Oatmeal," by Robert Johnson. *Challenge of the Heart*. Boston: Shambhala, pp. 18ff.

19. de Rougemont, Denis (1983). *Love in the Western World*, Translation by Montgomery Belgion; original copyright, 1940. Princeton: Princeton University Press, p. 15.

Hunt, Morton (1959). *The Natural History of Love*. New York: Alfred A. Knopf.

20. Fiedler, Leslie (1977). *A Fiedler Reader*. Critique of "Stony Sestina" written by Dante Alighieri. New York: Stein and Day, pp. 74ff; p. 96.

21. Lagerkvist, Par (1954). *The Marriage Feast*. New York: Hill and Wang (division of Farrar, Straus and Giroux), p. 15.

22. Welwood, John (Ed.) 1985. Ch. "Learning to Love," Rainer Maria Rilke, *Challenge of the Heart*. Boston: Shambhala, p. 262.

23. Rilke, Rainer Maria (1982). "Requiem," *The Selected Poetry*. Translation by Stephen Mitchell. New York: Random House, line 232, p. 306.

24. Bianchi, Eugene (1982). *Aging as a Spiritual Journey*, citing W. B. Yeats. New York: Crossroad Publishing Co., p. 130.

25. Shelton, Charles, S. J. (1983). *Adolescent Spirituality*. Chicago: Loyola University Press, pp. 8ff.

26. Moore, John (1980). *Sexuality and Spirituality*. San Francisco: Harper and Row, Publishers, Intro.

27. Fuchs, Eric (1983). *Sexual Desire and Love*. New York: The Seabury Press, Theses, pp. 219-231.

28. *Ibid*. V/3/5/6, p. 231.

29. Barnhouse, Ruth and Urban Holmes (Eds.) (1976). *Male and Female*, ch. by Norman Pittenger. New York: Seabury Press, p. 160.

30. Moore, John (1980). *Sexuality and Spirituality*, pp. 20, 21.

31. Watts, Alan (1958). *Nature, Man, and Woman*, pp. 142-146.

32. Hunt, Morton (1959). *The Natural History of Love*. New York: Alfred Knopf, pp. 91ff.

33. Chia, Mantak written with Michael Winn (1984). *Taoist Secrets of Love*. New York: Aurora Press, intro. iii-v.

34. Welwood, John (Ed.) (1985). Ch. by Suzanne Lilar, "The Sacred Dimension," *Challenge of the Heart*. Boston: Shambhala, pp. 229, 230.

35. Sittler, Joseph (1986). *Gravity and Grace*. Minneapolis: Augsburg Publishing House, pp. 25, 31.

36. Rilke, Rainer Maria (1982). "Duino Elegies IX," *The Selected Poetry*. New York: Random House, p. 123.

37. Sittler, Joseph (1986). *Gravity and Grace*, p. 123.

38. Nelson, James (1983). *Between Two Gardens*: Reflections on Sexuality and Religious Experience. New York: Pilgrim Press, p. 5.

39. Sittler, Joseph. *Gravity and Grace*, p. 123.

40. Erikson, Erik (1982). *The Life Cycle Completed*. New York: W. W. Norton and Co., p. 61.

41. *New English Bible*, Ecclestiasticus 25:1,2.

42. Shacochis, Bob. "Thighs and Whispers," *Vogue* (Feb. 1987). Beverly Hills: Conde Nast Publications, p. 390.

43. Fox, Matthew (1981). *Wheel We, Wee All the Way Home*: A Guide to Sensual, Prophetic Spirituality. Sante Fe: Bear and Co., p. 186.

44. Nouwen, Henri J. M. (1986). *Lifesigns*: Intimacy, Fecundity, and Ecstasy in Christian Perspective. Garden City: Doubleday, p. 27.

45. Montague, Ashley (1971). Citing study by Dr. Marc Hollander, *Touching*. New York: Columbia University Press, p. 165.

46. Prather, Hugh (Jan., Feb., 1987). *New Realities*, Vol. VII/3. "Growing Old Together." pp. 50, 51.

47. Kavanaugh, James (1985). "Serene Old Lady of the Afternoon," *Will You Still Love Me?* San Francisco: Argonaut Publishing, p. 57.

Wholistic Theology
as a Conceptual Foundation
for Services for the Oldest Old

Rev. James W. Ellor, DMin, AM, CSW, ACSW
Jane M. Thibault, PhD, CSW
F. Ellen Netting, PhD, ACSW
Catherine B. Carey, MA

SUMMARY. Social service agencies are focusing more and more on the "old-old." Some organizations have secular missions that address multiple domains (i.e., physiological, economic, social, etc.). Other agencies, developed by the religious community, designate spirituality as a domain to be addressed in serving the "old-old." This paper examines interfaces between secular social service organizations and those persons (whether staff, board or religious leaders) who attempt to provide a wholistic perspective for service provision to the "old-old."

The need to assert a wholistic perspective and the need to meet the challenge of service provision often clash when policy is made in the social service agency. Conflicts occur because the decisions regarding policy may reflect the collective theological stance of

Rev. James W. Ellor is Chair, Department of Human Services, and Coordinator of Gerontology Programs, National College of Education, 1 S. 331 Grace Street, Lombard, IL 60148. Jane M. Thibault is Assistant Professor, Department of Family Practice, University of Louisville, School of Medicine, Louisville, KY 40292. F. Ellen Netting is Assistant Professor, Arizona State University, School of Social Work, Tempe, AZ 85287. Catherine B. Carey is Executive Director, Visiting Nurse Association North, Evanston, IL 60202.

This paper was originally presented at the Conference on Aging and Wholeness at the School of Theology at Claremont, Claremont, CA, April 24, 1987. Research in this article was funded by the Retirement Research Foundation.

board members and agency personnel. However, decisions regarding active service provision may not always be able to reflect a wholistic stance, due to financial insufficiency or constraints imposed by funding sources. This conflict becomes more severe whenever the agency has an implied rather than a documented statement of values or theological foundation.

Wholistic perspectives and the challenges of service provision meet, and often clash, when policy is established in the social service agency. The decisions that shape policy and service provision may reflect the collective theology of the decision makers. Frequently this lack of congruence is overcome by the constraints of the regulations placed by funding sources and by a lack of sufficient funds to provide a particular service. Boards and policy makers which have not articulated a statement of values or a document that outlines the underlying theology involved in the services provided by their agency may be always subject to the vicissitudes of funding services.

THE BACKGROUND CONTEXT

When social workers reflect on the philosophical foundations of service provision, they pay attention to the ethical stance of service provision, since ethics provide the necessary set of rules for appropriate behavior. Informing these rules should be values that spawn the ethical position. However, an even more profound reality can be revealed when a theological position is considered.

Pherigo defines theology as, "faith seeking understanding."[1] While theology asserts that there are limits to the degree of insight which can be obtained by humanity, theologians continually attempt to articulate issues of belief, faith, and the human condition. The human condition is the theological concern that relates to social service provision. Whether or not it is acknowledged, the services that we provide reflect our views of human nature. If our society values older adults, then it must be prepared to provide the potential for their needs to be met. Unfortunately, our society reflects its negative views of aging every time it fails to provide the resources needed to address the needs of older adults. This point can be made dramatically by contrasting the widely publicized statements attributed to Governor Lamb of Colorado and Maggie Kuhn, an advocate of the aged. Governor Lamb suggested that, "it is the obligation of older persons and persons with terminal illness to die." Maggie Kuhn stated that, "We are not 'senior citizens' or 'golden agers.' We are the elders, the experienced ones; we are maturing, growing adults responsible for the survival of our society. We are not wrinkled babies, succumbing to trivial, purposeless waste of our years and time."[2] Obviously, the social services provided to reflect Governor Lamb's statement would be different from those that suggest support of Maggie Kuhn. There is always a particular view of the human condition which shapes the ethics and values of decisions.

A different example is demonstrated in the way that the social work profession suggests that a primary value is to honor the "individual's freedom of self determination."[3] This value yields such ethical statements as, "A Social worker should not put his or her own perceptions of a situation on the client." Supporting this value/ethics statement is a view of human nature that suggests that people are capable of insight into their own condition. In contrast, if one takes the common theological position that only God truly knows who we are, and what we need, then the assumption of self insight may be called into question. This concept is most evident when we attempt to serve the oldest old.

NEEDS OF THE OLDEST OLD

The Oldest Old includes all those persons who are over the age of 85. As a group they have increased 165% from 1960-1982.[4] By the year 2050, this sector will constitute 5% of the total population in the United States.[5] The concept of the "old old" was developed by Bernice Neugarten as a research technique to isolate the needs of the young-old.[6] The designation of 65-75 and 75+ has been in the literature since the mid 1970s. In the last 5 years people older than 85 have been identified as having different lifestyle requirements which policy makers must address separately.

There is very little in the gerontological literature describing the needs of the oldest old. However, recent summaries of census data allow us to portray this interesting group.

Among the oldest old, there are only 40 men for every 100

women.[7] The median income of persons over 85 is less than any other group of seniors, $13,750 for family units as compared to $19,774 for persons 65-74. Among women over the age of 85, 1 in five were recorded as living below the poverty level in 1984. Women have always been over represented among the elderly poor. This same study found that 60 percent of persons over the age of 65 were women, however, 71.1% of the persons who are poor are female.[8] While not every person in this age group is physically impaired, the potential for someone who is over the age of 85 to have physical disabilities, particularly chronic disabilities, is greater than for any other age group. "Males and females 85 and older are four times more likely to be disabled than those age 65-74. Almost half, about 46 percent, of persons 85-plus are mildly to severely disabled compared to about 13 percent of persons age 65 to 74, and 25 percent of persons 75-84 . . . about 12 percent of women in the oldest age category are severely disabled compared to less than 8 percent of men."[9]

When we examine mental health, the oldest old are less likely to suffer from functional disorders such as depression than are their young old counterparts. However, this same group is considerably more likely to suffer from Alzheimer's Disease.[10] Most persons over the age of 85 have fewer family and non-family support persons when compared to persons between the ages of 65-74. In one study, 40% of persons between 65-74 served by a visiting nurse association had some type of assistance from friends and neighbors, while only 26.3 percent of the oldest old benefited from this type of assistance. Clearly the potential for the oldest old to have outlived their family and friends is a very real problem.[11] This same study found that the oldest old were more likely to live alone, 44.8% when compared to the young old, 26.6%. With regard to home health services, Ellor found that the oldest old utilized slightly more services from registered nurses, (96.2% for young old, 98.7% among oldest old).[12] However, the number of patients seen by home health aides rises from 2.45% (young old) to 31.2% (oldest old). While services from such rehabilitation oriented disciplines as physical therapy, occupational therapy, and speech therapy decline with age, the oldest old are much more likely to utilize the services of companions, nurse aides, and chore services. Clearly, the oldest old are much more likely to utilize services that reflect chronic physical conditions than are their younger counterparts. Indeed, the oldest old consume very few rehabilitation services.

When we examine nursing homes, 2% of those 65-74 years live in nursing homes while 16% of the oldest old live in such facilities.[13] Senator Heinz concludes, "Those 85 and older have a three-fold greater risk of losing their independence, seven times the chance of entering a nursing home and two-and-a-half times the risk of dying compared to persons 65-74 years of age."[14]

THEOLOGICAL ISSUES FOR SERVING THE OLDEST OLD

Many authors have debated the question, should we have a theology of aging, or should we have a theology of life, one that supports positive aging? Given the overwhelming incidence of chronic physical illness, loss of familiar people, and potential for dependence in the later stages of old age, it is useful to consider this group in terms of their specific needs. Due to the unique challenges of the final years, the development of a theology of aging for the oldest old is appropriate and useful.

Theology takes varying positions on the maintenance of self. Some schools indicate that we all belong to God, and must turn to him for the assurance of continuity. Other theologians suggest that this task is accomplished by interaction with the community of faith which should be available at all times for this type of support.

The foundational value for services that address the needs of the oldest old reflect wholistic needs. The concept of Wholism is not new. Adler talks of taking a holistic view of the needs of clients as early as the 1920s. More recently, Granger Westberg brought forth the concept of the "Wholistic" approach to meeting health needs. While many different authors have conceptualized this philosophy differently, they have one thing in common. All of the authors discuss the nature of the person as having several different aspects or dimensions. These include the emotional self, the physical self, the social self, and the "fourth dimension" or the spiritual self added by Granger Westberg.

Each of the four dimensions can be conceptualized as separate entities. The psychologist can address the emotions, the recreation therapist can deal with the social, the physician can heal the body, and the clergyperson can minister to the soul. The important contribution of Alfred Adler was to point out that it is difficult to try to address each of these dimensions as if the others did not exist. The concept of wholism advocates the inclusion of all four dimensions in any assessment or treatment approach.

While the inclusion of all four dimensions is important, the functional question for persons providing services is, "How do we integrate the various aspects of the person into service?" The social worker or clergyperson is not a physician or nurse. Thus, they are often reluctant to delve too far into the medical needs of seniors. The need is for sensitivity and possible referral to persons who specialize in areas with which the practitioner is not as familiar.

Possibly the most difficult question when attempting to discuss a wholistic philosophy is the nature of the integration of the various aspects of the person. How do the four dimensions fit together? A review of the literature suggests that there are three different views regarding the integration of the four dimensions.[15] Most often the four are simply perceived as separate. Much like four pieces of a pie, they can be separated and addressed one at a time. A service that would reflect such a philosophy might be a medical clinic, where if the individual needed medical care she/he would see a physician. If s/he needed emotional counseling, s/he would move down the hall to the psychologist, and the same for a chaplain or recreation therapist. The clinic could claim to be wholistic because all the needed services were available. Yet the burden in this model for integration is on the patient.

A second concept suggests that one of the dimensions is foundational to the other three. Thus for example the medical community might argue that without the physical, the other three would not exist. Thus, the foundation for the person is his or her physical self. To operationalize this philosophy, an agency might hire physicians or nurses to do all of the services from counseling to prayer.

The final perspective would argue that one of the various aspects of the person provides an integrative force for the person, permeating all others. Thus, the focal dimension could not be separated from the other three, but rather provide the glue that integrates and holds together the other aspects of the person. Thus a service might see the emotional aspect to be the integrative force. If this is the case, the counselor would work to facilitate intellectual and emotional integration with his or her client.

The authors would agree with the National Interfaith Coalition who note, "The Spiritual is not one dimension among many in life; rather, it permeates and gives meaning to all life."[16] A wholistic philosophy would acknowledge and attempt to address the needs of all four aspects of the person, yet it would understand that it is the spiritual dimension that holds the individual together, providing an integrative force in the lives of people. This means that wholistic agencies would not only need to address the spiritual needs of clients, in the sense of giving them rides to worship, but rather, it would mean interacting with the client, facilitating the articulation and insight into the nature of the spirit, and the role of the spiritual in helping to integrate life.

Techniques such as spiritual life review and other methods that allow the individual to express his or her life in terms of a relationship with God, Self and other persons in the environment would be essential elements. A wholistic approach would also require conscious examination of other theological principles that are pertinent to the specific needs that pertain to their current stage in life. Four important issues merit discussion in this paper with regard to the oldest old. These are, "preparation for dying," "coping with chronic illness," "coping with dependency," and "expressing the potential for spiritual development."

Gerontologists have consistently suggested that coping with the fear of death is more of a middle aged task, rather than one for old age. Yet it is clear that by the time that one reaches eighty-five years of age, death is imminent. For the oldest old there is constant loss of old friends and even children who are themselves over the age of 65. Sensitivity to the needs of this group requires both an understanding of the meaning systems that constitute comfort for the oldest old in terms of the presence or absence of an after life, as well as an understanding of the need for stability in interpersonal relations.

Practitioners don't always consider this need for stability to be an issue with death. However, it is clear that seniors turn to their church or synagogue, not just for comfort, but also because they have been told that God, if not the church, will always be with them. At the time in life when one's meaning system is an important part of the perspective on death, it is also needed as a source of stability. Unfortunately stability is not enhanced when churches and synagogues make changes ranging from the introduction of a new hymnal to the major changes involved in Vatican II.

Possibly one of the most critical issues for the oldest old is the need to cope with the emotional changes involved in chronic illness. One of the most difficult changes that frequently accompanies later life is the fact that for the first time the body becomes unreliable! The issue for this age group is that many of the illnesses will never change. The related suffering and pain that goes with this type of illness is not consistent with both the expectations for activity held by society, or even the need to be active that many individuals maintain.

One of the problems faced by the person who is enduring chronic illness is the fact that in our society we are better at saying "I love you," or "I care about you," when people do things for us. We reward activity in the Judeo-Christian ethic by saying thank you, and in effect letting people know that they are needed by response to their actions. When they are unable to perform any type of activity, there is then the potential to feel that one is also not needed or even loved. A theology of understanding and supporting the chronically ill needs to be able to say, "I love you" just for being you, not for what you can do.

The next area of concern is reflected in the functional dependence that often comes with advanced age. For many seniors there is contradiction between the physical need for dependence, and the emotional need for independence. Particularly in light of the multiple chronic illnesses, and the fact that spouses are less likely to be the caretakers of the oldest old, they will need to depend on their children, grandchildren and even strangers for assistance to do things that for many years they could do for themselves.

Within the Judeo-Christian tradition, we have developed a social norm that in order to be dependent, one also has to be visibly sick. It is O.K. in our society to be dependent if one is sick enough. However, if the senior is not visibly sick, or is in need of dependency for emotional reasons, it is less acceptable to be dependent.[17] Any wholistic theology for the oldest old must include an understanding of dependence that is supportive of both emotional as well as physical needs. It will also need to support the person who is refusing to be dependent, when dependence is clearly justifiable!

Finally, we need to look upon the oldest old as a group that does continue to be both capable of and responsive to continued spiritual growth. Spiritual growth may be perceived by the senior as more difficult when everything else around him or her is changing and becoming more difficult. However, if the institutions around the senior cuts him or her off from potential growth, or assume that the senior is either uninterested or unwilling to participate, we are locking him or her into that which is not inevitable. The theological values needed for working with the oldest old must begin with the expectation that continued spiritual growth is both possible and desirable for the continued well being of the elderly.

The factor in a wholistic theology for the oldest old that encompasses the issues raised is the role of the spirit. It is the position of the authors that the spiritual dimension of the person is the aspect that is able to facilitate the type of integration that facilitates comfort with life upon reflection, interpretation of those aspects of life that are less comforting, and provides a sense of a bigger picture. The spiritual dimension is the integrator, the spirit is the integrating force in the life of any individual. The spirit is the interpreter of the greater whole of life; is able to support the individual in growth and in the interpretation of life.

Service delivery to the oldest old will need to take into consideration the points presented above. Agencies that fail to allow for struggles with dependency, or fear of death and chronic illness, will constantly be placed in a position to discontinue services for persons who no longer meet acute criteria, but continue to need the emotional support for chronic illness and emotional needs. The difficulty is that it is more expensive to provide services for chronic problems. When agencies are unable to serve adequately the acute needs of patients and are unable to find financial support for the chronic illnesses, they will find it difficult to justify the expenditure of funds for the on-going support of the oldest old. This may mean that there will be a greater need to support the informal systems in care for the oldest old.

PROGRAM EXAMPLES

The challenge of meeting the needs of the oldest old can not be understated. However models of potential programs do exist. Two programs that reflect a wholistic approach to the spiritual needs of the oldest old, as well as the values necessary to work with the oldest old are, "the Contemplative Community"[18] and "Senior Friends."[19] The Contemplative Community reflects an ideological congregation of persons coming together for spiritual growth and physical support. The physical surroundings of this group are similar to any other congregate living situation. The group would live in a facility that is both handicapped accessible and homelike. While some support for the activities of daily living would need to be available, the group would be expected to help each other as much as possible, providing as many of the meal preparation and house keeping tasks themselves as possible.

There are models for such a community. It follows the concept of "late vocations within the Catholic tradition where some older people enter the convent or monastery."[20] Also, in the spiritual development of Eastern religions there is a phase of house-holding where people are expected to be engaged in the everyday activities of daily life. In later life, these persons leave the activities of everyday life to seek God and to find meaning. The older adult contemplative community provides a sheltered care setting for persons who wish to support emotionally and spiritually each other's growth. This type of faith community can facilitate the integration of life and spirit for persons who struggle with physical disabilities.

The second program, Senior Friends, reflects a system of care and concern for the homebound. This group of seniors may be sponsored by a religious congregation, or any other group of concerned persons. It is composed of older adults who visit those returning home from the hospital. They begin with prayer, then inquire as to the needs of the homebound senior. If the person needs transportation, one or two of the seniors provides a ride in their car. (Ambulance or Medicare transportation is outside of the capabilities of this group.) If the person needs meals, all of the persons in the congregation are put on a list of providers. This list is coordinated by the seniors' group so that each family in the congregation provides a meal for the homebound senior once or twice a year, depending on the size of the congregation. If the person needs a companion, one of the Senior Friends will move in with the homebound person for a temporary period. Yet almost any service need can be met by this group without the exchange of money. Key to the success of the program is that when the homebound senior becomes well, he or she is expected to contribute to the group. Even if the person is still homebound, s/he is expected to assist with telephone communication or some other service. The most significant activity for group cohesion is the traveling Bible Study. The main group of seniors providing service move from one home of the homebound members to another holding their Bible Study in each home with the homebound member. This provides the homebound person with fellowship and allows the group to continue to check in with the senior to monitor need.

Both of these programs are directed at the physically impaired senior. While not all of the oldest old are health impaired, many are. Both of these programs address the needs of seniors for fellowship, physical support, and the assistance to continue to grow emotionally and spiritually.

CONCLUSION

The oldest old as a group have specific needs that are somewhat different from their younger cohorts. Service to this group needs to begin with a wholistic theology that can facilitate the human needs of these persons without denying that they are a part of the community of faith. In the absence of an articulated theological position that acknowledges the specific needs of the oldest old, service delivery will continue to be less than wholistic.

NOTES

1. Pherigo, Lindsey P., "Theological Issues and Aging." *Quarterly Papers on Religion and Aging.* (Vol. III, No. 2, Winter 1987) P. 1.

2. Hessel, Dieter, (ed) *Maggie Kuhn on Aging*, (Philadelphia, The Westminster Press, 1977).

3. Reamer, Frederick G. "Fundamental Ethical Issues in Social Work: An Essay Review," *Social Service Review*. (June 1979), P. 229.

4. Taeuber, C.M., *American in Transition: An Aging Society*, (Washington, D.C.: U.S. Department of Commerce, Bureau of the Census, Current Population Reports, Special Studied Series, No. 128, 1983).

5. Green, Roberta R., *Social Work with the Aged and their Families*, (Hawthorne, New York, Aldine de Gruyter, 1986), P. 189.

6. Neugarten, Bernice L. (Ed.) "Age Groups in American Society and the Rise of the Young-Old," *Political Consequences of Aging*. (Philadelphia: American Academy of Political and Social Sciences) PP. 187-198.

7. Heinz, John, *Developments in Aging: 1985*, (S. Res. 85, Sec. 19, February 28, 1985). Washington D.C.: U.S. Government Printing Office, P. 16.

8. Ibid, P. 38.

9. Ibid, P. 66.

10. Ellor, James W., *Home Health Services for the Oldest Old*, (Unpublished manuscript prepared for the Gerontological Society of America, 1987).

11. Ibid, P. 48.

12. Ibid.

13. Heinz, Ibid, P. 73.

14. Heinz, Ibid. P. 75.

15. Ellor, James W., "Bridging Churches and Social Service Agencies: Value Conflicts and Program Potential," *Social Work and Christianity*, 1983, Vol. 10, No. 1, P. 26.

16. National Interfaith Coalition on Aging, "Spiritual Well-Being," In *Spiritual Well-Being of the Elderly*. Edited by James A. Thorson, and Thomas C. Cook, Springfield, Illinois: Charles C. Thomas Publisher, 1980.

17. Miller, Michael, B., Schumacher, Frederick J., "The Aged, The Judeo-Christian Ethic, and Misuse of Illness for Dependency Needs" found in *Spiritual Well-Being of the Elderly*, Ed. by James A. Thorson and Thomas C. Cook, (Springfield, Illinois: Charles C Thomas Press, 1980) PP. 113-126.

18. Thibault, Jane M., "The development of a contemplative Community for Older Adults," Unpublished paper presented in roundtable discussion at the Gerontological Society of America, 1982.

19. Ellor, James W., Tobin, Sheldon S., "Beyond Visitation: ministries to the Homebound Elderly," *The Journal of Pastoral Care*, 1985 39 PP. 12-21.

20. Netting, F.E., Thibault, J.M., Ellor, J.W., "Spiritual Integration: Gerontological Interface Between the Religious and Social Service Communities," (Unpublished paper, delivered to the Southern Gerontological Society, April 1987).

Aging and the Search for Meaning

Melvin A. Kimble, PhD

SUMMARY. The natural science model is not adequate alone to deal with some of the profound problems of gerontology because it does not deal well with meaning and values issues. This paper develops the topic "Aging and the Search for Meaning" using phenomenological and hermeneutical methods. It is assumed that finding a meaning in life is a primary drive across the years. Such a quest requires a hermeneutic, i.e. a means by which life may be symbolized or given meaning and direction. Using Viktor Frankl's meaning theory, the paper introduces an approach which describes the process by which the meaning of aging can be interpreted.

Albert Camus once contended, "There is but only one truly serious problem, and that is . . . judging whether life is or is not worth living."[1] That basic, fundamental "problem" emerges with considerable urgency as persons become aged. Is growing old worth one's whole life to attain? What is the meaning of life when one is elderly? Can the meaning of whom I have become be sustained in this last stage of my life? To respond to these questions requires more than a biomedical paradigm.

There is an imperative need for a wider frame of reference in the study of aging that allows for the full exploration of the question of meaning in old age. The biological model used in gerontology, it has been stressed, is not adequate to explore and create new dimensions for understanding the meaning of growing and being old.

Melvin A. Kimble is affiliated with the Luther Northwestern Theological Seminary, 2481 Como Avenue, St. Paul, MN 55108.

111

Since World War II a vast empirical literature of gerontology has grown up. The dominant methodology in that literature has been inspired by a positivistic view of the natural and social sciences, a view that makes it difficult even to think of meaning as a legitimate object of inquiry.[2]

The natural science model has in many respects served gerontology well, but not well enough. It is powerless to reveal to us the meaning of our own lives. What is required is a concern for hermeneutics, not simply statistics; for understanding, not simply predicting. What is called for is an approach to aging and its processes that moves beyond an empirical research model which is limited to a positivistic focus in bio-medical and social conditions of aging.

This paper attempts to develop the topic "Aging and the Search for Meaning" by setting forth a phenomenological approach to gerontology utilizing hermeneutical methods. The writer accepts a priori that striving to find a meaning in life is a primary force throughout one's life span. The human experience of aging is here seen as requiring a hermeneutic, "a means whereby it may be symbolized, given meaning and direction."[3] Using meaning theory as formulated most particularly by Viktor Frankl,[4] it introduces a hermeneutical, phenomenological approach to describe the process by which the meaning of aging and growing old can be interpreted. In doing this it seeks to take seriously Michel Philibert's call for a third stage of gerontology:

> Human aging is a complex process whose biological conditions are embedded in and modified by a social and cultural, which is to say symbolic, context. One cannot study aging independently of the images, naive or sophisticated, in which it is expressed and constituted. The images require our investigation largely through the mediation of the disparate texts which express them, comment on them, or convey them. Gerontology was dominated in the first stage of its brief history by the doctors and the biologists. In a second stage, a place was created for the psychologists and the sociologists, flanked by some economists and demographers. Now gerontology is at the threshold of a third stage, and a period of renewal, based

upon the gathering of geographers, historians, linguists, exegetes, hermeneuticists, and semiologists around profound problems of aging.[5]

AGING AND THE CRISIS OF MEANING

It has been observed that the enormous gains in longevity through medical and technological progress have been accompanied ". . . by widespread spiritual malaise . . . and confusion over the meaning and purpose of human life — particularly in old age."[6] This experience of a sense of emptiness and meaninglessness has been discovered in the elderly populations not only of the United States but of different nations.[7] Global statistics seem to confirm Frankl's observation that "The truth is that as the struggle for survival has subsided, the question has emerged: *survival for what*? Ever more people today have the means to live but no meaning to live for."[8] Human beings do not live by welfare services or social security benefits alone! The crisis of old age appears to be a crisis of meaning.

Frankl maintains that "the feeling of meaninglessness, the existential vacuum is increasing and spreading to the extent that, in truth, it may be called a mass neurosis."[9] Such a neurosis describes the experience of a total lack or loss of an ultimate meaning to one's existence that would make life worthwhile. In older persons, this state of inner emptiness may well be one of the causes of depression and despair that contributes to the extraordinarily high suicide rate among the elderly, especially among older men following retirement.[10] In one research study, for example, the research team emphasized that in order effectively to help depressed people, ". . . *the ultimate answer would be for old age itself to offer the elderly something worthwhile for which to live.*"[11]

There appears to be an absence of symbols of transcendence in our society that would provide answers to the questions related to meaning of aging and growing old. For that reason it is not surprising that the irrational and anxious dread about growing old has manifested itself increasingly at much earlier stages of the human life cycle than one would normally expect. The fortieth, and even the thirtieth birthday, are celebrated with a fearful foreboding of what lies ahead. What should be experienced as the prime of life is often already being experienced as a decline. Contributing to this grimness about aging is a conspicuous lacuna of symbols and appropriate rituals to mark and give positive meaning to the passing of life time.

Without positive symbols that give meaning to growing old, it is understandable why aging is viewed as a "medical problem." Medical science, itself, has been guilty of reinforcing this negative view by sometimes treating aging as a disease to be prevented or cured. The plethora of publications by medical authors with such titles as *No More Dying: The Conquest of Aging and the Extension of Human Life*[12] and *Prolongevity*[13] suggest that medical technology has the potential not only to extend life but even to abolish death. Anti-aging research programs generate bold claims such as "Old age will be a disease you can go to see your doctor about, if, indeed, prophylactic measures do not virtually eradicate it."[14]

The resultant viewing of aging as pathological and as an avoidable or preventable affliction represents a further massive erosion of positive images and meanings concerning growing old and being aged. It generates a predictable glorification of youthfulness and an irrational denial of aging as a natural process of life that ends in death. In other words, it negates the meaning of being old. A society that invests so much psychic energy in avoiding aging and denying death manifests the symptoms of symbolic retardation with its resultant impoverishment of meaning concerning the human experience of aging and dying.

HERMENEUTICAL PHENOMENOLOGY AND AGING

Hermeneutics, broadly speaking, is the art and science of interpretation. Throughout life, at every stage, the developing self is confronted with the necessity of making interpretations and assigning meanings to what is experienced. A myth or story is fashioned from the cultural images and language transmitted by significant others and the experience of being a self separate from other selves. The individual, as Gerkin asserts, is the hermeneut or myth maker, and from our individual mythic stories new experiences are anticipated and given meaning.[15] The hermeneutical perspective is not concerned about predicting or controlling human behavior. In this sense it is radically different from the methodology of empirical science. Its aim is to describe what is observed and thereby to further understanding.

Phenomenology focuses on the importance of the individual as one who is actively and intentionally seeking meaning in the midst of his or her contextual, social, cultural lived world. It examines the individual person and views that person as an active, self-reflecting, self-constructing person embedded in a social, cultural, and historical context. As Spigelberg states, "A hermeneutic phenomenology tries to interpret the meaning of the phenomena, especially that of human *Dasein*."[16]

Frankl states that phenomenology "speaks" the language of man's pre-reflective self-understanding rather than interpreting a given phenomenon after preconceived patterns."[17] Phenomenology is an example of a method conceptualized within the hermeneutic perspective. The task of phenomenology, according to Frankl, is to ". . . translate the wisdom of the heart into scientific terms."[18]

By the method of hermeneutic phenomenology older persons become our teachers through their own experience of aging. Phenomenologic hermeneutics is the revolt against the attempt to replace the world of every day experience by a system of meanings organized by science. It attempts to balance understanding of reality by recognizing the role of the subject in perception — by analyzing the relationship between the subject and the world. It cuts through the conflict between idealism and empiricism by stressing the relationship between the subject and the world — that to try to understand how a person "knows" apart from a person as "subject-in-the-world" is an impossibility. It studies the nature and structure of consciousness and is concerned with subjective reality. As Reker states, "It seeks to express explicitly the implicit structure and meaning of human experience."[19]

A hermeneutical phenomenology views individuals as conscious and active, and as capable of symbolization and symbol manipulation. Suzanne Langer has described the symbol making function "as one of man's primary activities, like eating, looking, or moving about . . . the fundamental process of his mind . . . essential to thought and prior to it."[20] In a similar vein, Frankl has stressed that

"Man is the being who is capable of creating symbols, and a being in need of symbols."[21] By symbolization we are able to represent our environments and thereby exercise existential choices that include alternative constructions and revisions or even replacements. Our ability to symbolize allows us to transcend time boundaries, to reminisce about our past and anticipate the future. As we pass through time, we interpret all of life's events and construct our "reality."

THE NATURE OF PERSONAL MEANING

The fundamental underlying postulate of this paper is that an individual throughout her or his life-span is motivated to seek and to find personal meaning in human existence.[22] The process by which the individual creates a sense of personal meaning can be understood within the framework of Viktor Frankl's logotherapy and my elaboration and application of it to the last stage of life. Frankl asserts that striving to find meaning in our life is our primary motivational force throughout the life-cycle and that is a universal human motive. Ross Snyder agrees and further states:

> Meaning formation is a central activity of the species "Human Being." The vitality—and graciousness—of a person's life depends upon their supply of meanings. Particularly in the second half of life. Meaning formation is not a fringe benefit, but a major ministry to people in the last half of life. A major way these years stay freshly human. A next step in developing the field of Gerontology is concentration of Meaning Formation.[23]

The frustration of an individual's will to meaning, according to Frankl results in a certain type of neurosis which logotherapy has labelled "noogenic neurosis"; that is to say, a neurosis the origin of which is a spiritual problem, a moral conflict, or unrewarded search for an ultimate meaning to one's life.[24] A "noogenic neurosis" caused by a loss of meaning is characterized by boredom, depression, hopelessness, and the loss of a will to live. Frankl draws upon the spiritual resources of his patients by leaving the psychological dimension to enter the noological dimension, " . . . the dimension of a person's concern with, and search for, ultimate meaning."[25] According to Frankl, an ultimate meaning and purpose already exists in the world, but it must be personally discovered. It is not a matter of our intellectual cognition but rather the matter of our existential commitment.

Sources of Personal Meaning

Personal meanings do not develop in a vacuum. A phenomenological analysis of the immediate data of the actual life experience of an individual reveals sources of meaning in that person's life. Frankl maintains that life can be made meaningful in a threefold way:

> First, through *what we give* (in terms of our creative works); second, by *what we take* from the world (in terms of our experiencing values); and third, through *the stand we take* toward a fate we no longer can change (an incurable disease, an inoperable cancer, or the like).[26]

Meaning is not invented but is discovered. We can give meaning to our lives by realizing *creative* values, that is, by achieving tasks. We can also give meaning to our lives by realizing *experiential* values, "by experiencing the Good, the True and the Beautiful, or by knowing one single human being in all of his uniqueness. And to experience one human being as unique means to love him."[27] Even when these experiences are impossible, "a man can still give his life a meaning by the way he faces his fate, his distress."[28] A person realizes values by attitudes toward destined or inescapable suffering. These *attitudinal* values, as Frankl calls them, gives a person, when being confronted with a hopeless situation, a last opportunity to fulfill a meaning—"to realize even the highest value to fulfill even the deepest meaning—and that is the meaning of suffering."[29] It is a tenet of logotherapy that life's transitoriness does not in the least detract from its meaningfulness. Life holds meaning up until the last breath.

Self-Transcendence

Self-transcendence, according to logotherapy, is the essence of existence. Frankl explains:

> I thereby understand the primordial anthropological fact that being human is being always directed and pointing to something or someone other than oneself: to a meaning to fulfill or another human being to encounter, a cause to serve or a person to love. Only to the extent that someone is living out this self-transcendence of human existence, is he truly human or does he become his true self. He becomes so, not by concerning himself with his self's actualization, but by forgetting himself and giving himself, overlooking himself and focusing outward.[30]

Logotherapy underscores the fact that a person is a deciding being. The individual has both actuality and potentiality and exists as his or her own possibility. The freedom to choose and change is ever present in an individual's life. While acknowledging the limiting circumstances and conditions that are ever present in a person's life, Frankl writes:

> . . . Man is *not* fully conditioned and determined; he determines himself whether to give into conditions or to stand up to them. In other words, man is ultimately self-determining. Man does not simply exist, but always decides what his existence will be, what he will become in the next moment.[31]

The awareness of possibilities and the understanding that an individual is a deciding being conveys hope. Hope must be seen in relationship to freedom. To be free is to stand before possibilities. It is to transcend the present situation and see one's capacity to alter the status quo, even if limited to one's own attitude toward unavoidable suffering. Without such a concept of freedom, there can be no hope. Frankl contends:

> Man is not "driven," man decides. Man is free, but we prefer to speak of responsibility instead of freedom. Responsibility implies something for which we are responsible, namely, the accomplishment of concrete personal tasks and demands, the realization of that unique and individual meaning which everyone of us has to fulfill.[12]

The individual remains responsible for the way he or she reshapes life in the future. The existential sovereignty of a person over his or her life is thereby affirmed. Potentialities for meaning are ever present in life. The emphasis on responsibility in logotherapy brings hope because it assumes that an individual has the freedom to alter and fashion one's life and thereby the future. In a sense it is one and the same thing to deprive a person of one's freedom, of one's future, and of one's hope. Frankl is concerned that the deterministic and reductionistic models of humankind are guilty of doing exactly this. The concepts of freedom and responsibility are the essentially human characteristics, and we are deprived of the uniqueness of our humanity when they are ignored or violated.

An illuminating summary of meaning confrontation is provided by Frankl:

> Once meaning orientation turns into meaning confrontation, that stage of maturation and development is reached in which freedom — that concept so much emphasized by existentialists' philosophy — becomes responsibleness. Man is responsible for the fulfillment of the specific meaning of his personal life. But he is also responsible *before* something, or *to* something, be it society, or humanity, or mankind, or his own conscience. However, there is a significant number of people who interpret their own existence not just in terms of being responsible to something but rather to someone, namely to God.[13]

Logotherapy's inclusion of a "supra-meaning" describes life's unconditional meaningfulness and the ultimate meaning that embraces all of life. Frankl reflecting on his role as a medical doctor writes:

> Day by day I am confronted with people who are incurable, men who become senile, and women who remain sterile. I am besieged by their cry for an answer to the question of an ultimate meaning to suffering. . . . But if there is meaning, it is unconditional meaning, and neither suffering nor dying can detract from it. And what our patients need is conditional faith in unconditional meaning.[34]

PERSPECTIVES ON PERSONAL MEANING AND THE LIFE CYCLE

The Meaning of Time

A marked characteristic of logotherapy is that it takes time seriously. Its existential thrust stresses the temporal nature of human existence and the irreversible quality of human life. The individual is accepted as one responsible for his or her life story and the telling of it.

Memory implies time elapsed. In remembering an individual takes responsibility for values actualized and values denied. From time to time, for example, we must bear the pain of remembering ourselves as persons who denied or negated values closely identified with our self-image. Memories of the past sometimes reflect unfulfilled self-expectations. When potentialities are denied or left unfulfilled, we experience guilt. Not only are existential guilt and guilt feelings carried over from the past, but also the memory of certain positive and purposeful deeds and experiences and even the acceptance of some unavoidable suffering. Logotherapy's understanding of time is poignantly set forth by Frankl:

> All that is good and beautiful in the past is safely preserved in the past. On the other hand, so long as life remains, all guilt and all evil is still "redeemable". . . . This is not the case of a finished film . . . or an already existent film which is merely

being unrolled. Rather, the film of this world is just being "shot." Which means nothing more or less than that the future — happily — still remains to be shaped; that is, it is at the disposal of man's responsibility.[35]

Frankl's ontology of time holds that "having been" is still a mode of being, perhaps even the safest mode. Frankl provides another poignant image of time and its passing with his illustration of a man who:

> . . . observes with fear and sadness that his wall calendar, from which he daily tears a sheet, grows thinner with each passing day, . . . Has he any reason to envy the young people he sees . . . or wax nostalgic over his own lost youth? What reasons has he to envy a young person? The future that is in store for him? "No, thank you," he will think. "Instead of possibilities, I have realities in my past, not only the reality of work done and of love loved, but of suffering bravely suffered. These sufferings are the things of which I am most proud, though they are things which cannot inspire envy."[36]

Once a possibility has been made into a reality, it is delivered safely into "the granary of the past." But we have the responsibility for what we have selected to be deposited in the past, what should be eternalized. "The past is precisely that which cannot be taken away."[37]

Life Cycle

The development of changing values and meanings over the life course has been theorized by a number of life-span psychologists. Erik Erikson is best known for his linkage of societal values with developmental tasks to be accomplished.[38] Meanings for the adolescent, young, and middle aged adult are centered in establishing a stable identity, forming intimate relationships, and being productive and creative. The task of late life, the last stage, is to develop a sense of integrity, an appreciation of why and how one has lived. The common thread of these stages is that life unfolds with unique tasks to be accomplished at each stage. This epigenetic process includes the developmental tasks of integrating and transcending the experiences of a lifetime. Integration becomes a meaningful process. The implication of this, as Reker and Wong suggest, is that the meaning system of an individual will become increasingly more differentiated and integrated as a function of age. Frankl states:

> Since each situation is unique, with a meaning that is also necessarily unique, it now follows that the "possibility to do something about a situation" is unique also insofar as it is transitory. It has a "kairos" quality, which means that unless we use the opportunity to fulfill the meaning inherent and dormant in a situation, it will pass and be gone forever. Yet it is only the possibilities — the opportunities to do something about reality — that are transitory. Once we have actualized the possibility offered by a situation, once we have fulfilled the meaning a situation holds, we have converted that possibility into a reality, and we have done so once *and forever!*[39]

How a life has been lived, is lived, and will be lived make up the changing set of personal meanings over the life span. Frankl concedes that there is little indication of a will to meaning in the earliest stages of development. But this is understood as soon as it is recognized ". . . that life is a *Zeitgestalt*, a time gestalt, and as such becomes something whole only after the life course has been completed. A certain phenomenon may therefore form a constitutive aspect of humanness and yet manifest itself only in an advanced stage of development."[40]

Logotherapy reflects a dynamic understanding that in life the opportunities to address oneself to a particular group of values or meanings varies from hour to hour, from day to day, "Sometimes life demands of us the realization of creative values; at other times we feel it necessary to turn to the category of experiential values. . . . Sometimes the demands of the hour may be fulfilled by an act, at another time by our surrendering to the glory of an experience."[41] And, of course, there remains the opportunity to realize attitudinal values at every stage of life when confronted by a destiny towards which a person can act only by acceptance. "The way in which he accepts, the way in which he bears his cross, what courage he manifests in suffering, what dignity he displays in doom and disaster, is the measure of his human fulfillment."[42]

The Meaning of Death

Dying and suffering belong to the human condition. For Frankl, the tragic triad of pain, guilt, and death are inevitable and inherent in human existence.[43] but, according to logotherapy, it is this very transitoriness of human existence which constitutes an individual's responsibleness — the essence of existence. It is this two-fold understanding of finiteness in terms of fallibility and mortality which add to life's worthwhileness ". . . since only in the face of guilt does it make sense to improve, and only in the face of death is it meaningful to act."[44]

According to logotherapy, our own past is our true future. While we are alive, we have both a future and a past; the dying man has no future in the usual sense, but only a past; the dead, however, "is" his past. He has no life, he "is" his life. We become a reality, not at our birth, but rather at our death. We are "creating" ourselves at the moment of our death. Our self "is not something that 'is' but something that is becoming, and therefore becomes itself fully only when life has been completed by death."[45]

For logotherapy, the uniqueness of the person and the singularity of the situation are fundamental components of the meaning of human life. Human finiteness is present in both of these factors, and gives meaning to human existence. Consequently, a person's responsibility in life must be understood in terms of temporality and singularity.[46] Life is never an end in itself, but acquires meaning from other nonbiological frames of reference.[47] "Life transcends itself not in 'length' — in the sense of reproduction of itself — but in 'height' — by fulfilling values — or in 'breadth' in the community."[48]

Defiant Power of the Human Spirit

One of logotherapy's most helpful contributions to gerontology is its stress on the "defiant power of the human spirit." While recognizing the wholistic nature of the human being, the logotherapist appeals to what lies beyond the person's psycho-physical nature — the spirit. The spiritual core of a person is recognized as capable of taking a stand not only toward negative and painful external circumstances but also toward its own psychological character structure. Such recognition conveys to persons a renewed awareness of self worth and human dignity, and help them comprehend themselves as being fashioned "in the image of God." Conversely, if they regard themselves as inadequate psychic mechanisms, with no control and responsibility for themselves, they have no capacity to transcend themselves or fashion meaning from their suffering.[49]

Life Review as a Method of Mutual Ministry

Life review appears to be one of the developmental tasks of the last stage of life. There is a sense of urgency for the elderly to share their life story. One of the developmental tasks of aging is to maintain a past-scanning function that reclaims the past. Our personal experiences are always located in time. The fear of forgetting and the need to remember both mark the last stage of life. Memory enables us to hold fast to our identity and to shape and interpret it in new ways. We do not merely have these memories; we are these memories. By remembering we make connections and discover the patterns and designs of our lives. Life review provides a configuration, a mosaic of meaning in our lives, and facilitates the next stage which includes death. Life review, in other words, helps older adults tell their story, who they are and where they have been.

Frankl elaborates:

> Nothing and nobody can deprive and rob us of what we have safely delivered and deposited in the past. In the past nothing is irretrievably and irrecoverably lost but permanently stored. Usually people see only the stubblefield of transitoriness — they do not see the full granaries into which they have brought in the harvest of their lives: the deeds done, the works created, the loves loved, the sufferings courageously gone through.[49]

Life review is a normal activity that persons in every culture have engaged in and valued, for reminiscing by way of oral histories has recounted the past and provided cultural wisdom through the ages.

Dr. Robert Butler, beginning with a seminal article in 1963, introduced reminiscence as a form of life review as a therapeutic tool in the service of ego integrity for older people. Butler suggested that life review is a universal experience shared by all older persons albeit granting different intensities and results. Butler has written:

> As the past marches in review, it is surveyed, observed, and reflected upon by the ego. Reconsideration of previous experiences and their meanings occurs, often with concomitant revised or expanded understanding. Such reorganization of past experiences may provide a more valid picture, giving new and significant meanings to one's life. It may also prepare one for death, mitigating one's fears.[50]

Recent empirical studies have confirmed the value of life review with older adults. It has proven to help maintain a higher level of functioning, an increase in mental alertness, a greater sense of personal identity, and a reinforcement of coping mechanism.[51]

Life review is a phenomenological approach in seeking to understand the "lived world" of a person. It shifts away from a reductionistic analysis of the events of a person's life. It is more than a sentimental journey back through time; it is helping that person identify meanings in his or her own life. It means gently nudging persons to reflect on what a particular joyful or sorrowful event meant in their lives. It chronicles not only a person's encounter with life, but with God. It utilizes reminiscence as a tool for mutual ministry in assisting persons to become more aware of the continuity and meaning of their lives. The patterns of our lives are shaped by the meaning we give to what we remember.

The implications of life review for ministry are obvious and myriad. Memory reveals God's presence in our lives. Faith is the recounting of God's love and presence in our journey through time. Skilled ministry that understands the dynamics of life review can help older persons retrieve events from their memories that mediate God's graciousness to them. Furthermore, by the healing word of God's forgiveness conveyed to them, they escape the sense of despair caused by old guilts and failures that have continued to fester through time. Because emotional and spiritual options remain open until death, as both Butler and Frankl remind us, reconciliation and healing remain viable possibilities.

CONCLUSION

Religion has the inescapable challenge in this technocratic age to try to bring wholeness to older persons plagued with the brooding sense of emptiness which characterizes the *Krankheit des Zeitgeistes*, the sickness of our time. This essay has introduced selective descriptive elements in the logotherapeutic theory of Viktor Frankl which may in some positive fashion contribute to our thinking about religion and aging, especially aging and meaning formation. Logotherapy provides a theory and technique to meet the challenge and, from the boundary line of medicine, offers to share in this helping ministry.

Ministry with older adults will find in Logotherapy an ally in accessing the human situation and apprehending the totality and multidimensionality of the older person. The logotherapeutic tenet that self-transcendence is the essence of human existence opens the door to a deeper understanding of the human capacity to dedicate and devote one's self to something or someone beyond one's self. Logotherapy with its concept of dimensional ontology provides creative interpretations of the ontological differences and anthropological unity of personhood.[52] It enriches understanding of meanings and values, of freedom and responsibility, of decision and responsibleness, of suffering and faith. Logotherapy exegetes what Rheinhold Niebuhr has characterized as "the basic question of religion," namely, "the problem of meaning."[53] It dynamically focuses on what Tillich pointed to when he wrote: "Man is ultimately concerned about his being and his meaning."[54] Because it affirms faith and unconditional meaning, and because it boldly follows a person into the labyrinthian depths of the spiritual dimension, logotherapy helps Judeo-Christian ministry rediscover the multi-dimensionality of human nature.

In its recognition of the wholistic nature of the person. Frankl's model appeals to what lies beyond the psycho-physical nature of a person. This paradigm recognizes the spiritual dimension as the inclusive and encompassing dimension for understanding and integrating human phenomena. It circumscribes that which is not comprehensible in biology, psychology, and other disciplines. By emphasizing that a human being is not simply a psychosomatic organism, its phenomenological analysis introduces an understanding of personhood which affirms one's capacity to find meaning in life, indeed, even in suffering and dying. It is this unique spiritual capacity which conveys a renewed awareness of self worth and human dignity and assists persons in understanding themselves as fashioned in the image of God. While not intended to be a substitute or even a supplement for religion,[55] logotherapy provides an understanding of life at all of its stages, including old age, as life lived *sub specie aeternitatis*.

ENDNOTES

1. Albert Camus, *The Myth of Sisyphus* (New York: Vintage Books, 1955), p. 3.

2. Harry R. Moody and Thomas R. Cole, "Aging and Meaning: A Bibliographical Essay," eds. Thomas R. Cole and Sally A. Gadow, *What Does it Mean to Grow Old* (Durham: Duke University Press, 1986), p. 248.

3. Charles V. Gerkin, *Crisis Experience in Modern Life* (New York: Abingdon, 1979), p. 321.

4. Viktor Frankl, *Man's Search for Meaning: An Introduction to Logotherapy* (Boston: Beacon Press, 1959; paperback edition, New York: Pocket Books, 1977).

Frankl, *The Doctor and the Soul: From Psychotherapy to Logo- Therapy* (New York: Alfred Knopf, Inc.; second, expanded edition, 1965; paperback edition, New York: Vintage Books, 1978).

Frankl, *Psychotherapy and Existentialism: Selected Papers on Logotherapy* (New York: Washington Square Press, 1967; Touchstone paperback, 1975).

Frankl, *The Will To Meaning: Foundations and Applications of Logo-Therapy* (New York: The World Publishing Co., 1969; paperback edition, New York: New American Library, 1976).

Frankl, *The Unconscious God: Psychotherapy and Theology* (New York: Simon and Schuster, 1976).

5. Michel Philibert, "The Phenomenological Approach to Images of Aging," eds. Carol LeFevre and Perry LeFevre, *Aging and the Human Spirit* (Chicago: Exploration Press, 1981).

6. Thomas R. Cole, "Aging, Meaning, and Well-Being; Musings of a Cultural Historian," *International Journal of Aging and Human Development*, 19 (1984), p. 329.

7. Hiroshi Takashima, *Psychomatic Medicine and Logotherapy* (Oceanside, New York: Dabor Science Publications, 1977), 60.

8. Viktor Frankl, *The Unheard Cry for Meaning*, p. 21.

9. Ibid., p. 25.

10. Marv Miller, *Suicide After Sixty* (New York: Springer, 1979), pp. 11-12.

11. Ibid., p. 19.

12. Joel Kurtzman and Philip Gordon, *No More Dying: The Conquest of Aging and the Extension of Human Life* (Los Angeles: J.P. Tarcher, Inc.), 1976.

13. Albet Rosenfeld, *Prolongevity* (New York: Alfred Knopf, 1976).

14. Ibid., p. 218.

15. Charles, *The Living Human Document: Re-visioning Pastoral Counseling in a Hermeneutical Mode* (New York: Abingdon, 1984), pp. 20-21.

16. Herbert Spiegelberg, *Phenomenology in Psychology and Psychiatry* (Evanston: Northwestern University Press, 1972), p. xxix.

17. Viktor Frankl, *Psychotherapy and Existentialism*, p. 2.

18. Frankl, *The Unconscious God*, p. 131.

19. Gary T. Reker and Paul T. P. Wong, "Aging as an Individual Process: Toward a Phenomenological Theory of Human Development," unpublished paper.

20. Suzanne Langer, *Philosophy in a New Key* (Cambridge: Harvard University Press, 1942), p. 29.

21. Frankl, *The Will to Meaning*, p. 153.

22. Frankl, *Psychotherapy and Existentialism*. p. 72.

23. Ross Snyder, "Meaning Formation and Significant Survival," *Meaning and Senior Adults* (San Francisco Theological Seminary, San Anselmo, California, 1983), workshop handout.

24. Frankl, *Psychotherapy and Existentialism*, p. 122.

25. Frankl, *The Will to Meaning*, pg. 123.

26. Frankl, *Psychotherapy and Existentialism*, pg. 15.

27. Frankl, *The Doctor and the Soul*, p. xii.

28. Ibid.

29. Frankl, *Psychotherapy and Existentialism*, pp. 14-15.

30. Frankl, *The Unheard Cry for Meaning*, p. 35.

31. Frankl, *Man's Search for Meaning*, p. 206.

32. Frankl, *Psychotherapy and Existentialism*, p. 127.

33. Ibid., pp. 12-13.

34. Frankl, *The Will to Meaning*, pp. 155-156.

35. Frankl, *The Doctor and the Soul*, p. 27.

36. Frankl, *The Unheard Cry for Meaning*, pp. 104-105.

37. Ibid., p. 112.

38. Erik Erikson, *Identity and the Life Cycle* (New York: International Universities Press, 1959).

39. Frankl, *The Unheard Cry for Meaning*, p. 38.

40. Frankl, "Self Transcendence as a Human Phenomenon," *Journal of Humanistic Psychology*, VI, No. 2 (Fall, 1966), pp. 99-100.

41. Frankl, *Doctor and the Soul*, p. 36.

42. Ibid, pp. 35-36.

43. Ibid, p. 36.

44. Frankl, *Psychotherapy and Existentialism*, p. 88.

45. Frankl, *Unheard Cry for Meaning*, pp. 112-113.

46. Frankl, *Doctor and the Soul*, p. 55.

47. Ibid.

48 Melvin Kimble, "Application in Pastoral Psychology," *The International Forum for Logotherapy*, Vol. 2, No. 2, p. 33.

49. Frankl, *Unheard Cry for Meaning*, pp. 38-39.

50. Robert Butler, "The Life Review: An Interpretation of Reminiscence in the Aged," *Psychiatry*, 1963, 24, p. 68.

51. Irene Burnside, *Working with the Elderly*, (Monterey, California: Wadsworth, 1984), 2nd ed., pp. 298-307.

52. Frankl, *The Will to Meaning*, op. cit., pp. 22-30.

53. Rheinhold Niebuhr, *The Nature and Destiny of Man*, Volume I (New York: Charles Scribner, 1953), pg. 164.

54. Paul Tillich, *Systematic Theology*, Volume I (University of Chicago Press, 1951), pg. 22.

55. Frankl, *The Doctor and the Soul*, op. cit., pg. 245.

Authentic Humor as an Expression of Spiritual Maturity

Susan H. McFadden, PhD

SUMMARY. Erikson's understanding of ego integrity and Fowler's depiction of conjunctive faith provide theoretical insights into the holistic nature of spiritual maturity. In order to ground the theory in the actual experience of aging persons, this paper demonstrates how authentic humor represents an expression of spiritual maturity. Authentic humor can articulate the trust, hope and the faith of elders who maintain a sense of meaning and wholeness despite the changes, losses and suffering which often accompany the aging process. Persons who possess the resource of authentic humor experience the paradoxicalities of aging without yielding to despair.

The idea of spiritual maturity has strong intuitive appeal. Even those who have never heard the term nor considered its theoretical implications would probably be able to name persons they consider to be spiritually mature. This notion of spiritual maturity grasps those who consider it; it is a powerful idea which beckons us to discern its nature.

In order fully to understand spiritual maturity, we are best served if we use overdetermination, a process first described by Sigmund Freud and later defined by Erik Erikson as "a certain extravagance in searching for all possible relevances."[1] These "possible relevances" take many forms. First, seeking an adequate theoretical comprehension of spiritual maturity, we consider it from the perspectives of psychology and of faith. The horizontal dimension of spiritual maturity in human development invites the psychological

---

Susan H. McFadden is Assistant Professor of Psychology, University of Wisconsin—Oshkosh, Oshkosh, WI 54901.

131

approach. The vertical dimension, where the numinous is encountered, calls for an understanding of faith.

Theory alone, however, will not completely reveal the meaning of spiritual maturity. Spiritual maturity must not be reified in some ideal theoretical form far removed from human life. Rather, we should try to understand it phenomenologically, as embedded within human experience. Further, the search for manifestations of spiritual maturity directs us to a certain part of the life cycle both by our theoretical musings and also by our own encounters with persons who seem so fully to express it. We are led to old age.

With little effort we can doubtless name attributes of those older persons we consider to be spiritually mature: they demonstrate compassion, patience, generosity, wisdom. But something is missing from this list of attributes, something which Florida Scott-Maxwell expressed well when, at age 80, she wrote:

> I am getting fine and supple from the mistakes I've made, but I wish a notebook could laugh. Old and alone, one lives at such a high moral level. One is surrounded by eternal verities, noble austerities to scale on every side, and frightening depths of insight. It is inhuman. I long to laugh.[2]

Scott-Maxwell's reflections on aging reveal her to be a person of spiritual maturity. But why, we ask, does she long to laugh? What will her laughter mean to her? At what will she laugh? These questions point us to another: Can an understanding of spiritual maturity include humor as one of its attributes? Humor, we might argue, is too frivolous, too ephemeral, to be associated with a form of human experience which reaches toward the very horizon of mystery. Nevertheless, despite the dour testimony of much of the history of the Christian church regarding humor, humor can be interpreted as a vital ingredient in the constitution of spiritual maturity. This paper will demonstrate the congruence between what will be defined as authentic humor and the faith, hope and trust expressed by the spiritually mature.

UNDERSTANDING SPIRITUAL MATURITY

For the psychologist who attempts to comprehend the nature of spiritual maturity, the problem of definition looms large. The very words which form the idea — "spiritual" and "maturity" — immediately present challenges. For example, is it possible to understand spirituality apart from religiosity? Although the two are often associated, religiosity more often implies behaviors and beliefs which can be compartmentalized and intellectualized; religious behaviors and beliefs do not necessarily grasp the whole person, a point often emphasized by James Fowler in his work on faith development.

Spirituality, on the other hand, connotes for the modern mind a more wholistic description of what is essentially religious: the quest for ultimate meanings, values, and answers to questions like "For what purpose have I lived?" "Have my allegiances made a difference to anyone?" "How can I live knowing the inevitability of death?" These questions represent efforts to extract order from chaos, to seek the transcendent in the transient, and to comprehend at the deepest levels the self and the world. While organized religion offers structures of language, myth and ritual which enable many persons to encounter and even to resolve these issues, religious institutions can also impede the search for solutions to these questions by representing themselves as omniscient and powerful sources of religious "truths" uncritically accepted by their adherents. Further, when the aim of religious beliefs and behaviors is the fulfillment of infantile wishes and impulses, then the idea of "religious maturity" becomes an oxymoron.[3]

Conceptualizations of maturity present additional difficulties, for they are often fraught with popular meanings colored by unexamined socio-cultural assumptions. Maturity can be defined quantitatively in terms of a certain number of years lived or qualitatively as an indication of "mental health," "adjustment," "stability," "ego strength," and "self actualization." When maturity is associated with these variously depicted optimal states of being, not only do different theoretical world-views in psychology collide but also the value-laden nature of these terms is revealed. Reflecting on this, Richard Coan has written:

> Those qualities that are regarded as desirable, normal, or healthy in our society are likely at the same time to be the qualities that we associate with maturity . . . Our [American] notion of maturity embodies many of the ingredients of the good industrial citizen and owes much to the Protestant ethic.[4]

Another problem with the ambiguous notion of maturity is that it, like religion, can be experienced as an extrinsic, static quality of the self. Maturity in this sense becomes a patina of proper deportment, emotional reserve, and dedication to a task. The difficulty with this conception of maturity becomes most apparent when applied to the old. The elder who wishes to be playful, or to enjoy a sexual relationship, or to take some risks may be denigrated as lacking maturity.

The problematic nature of "religion" and "maturity" as popularly understood centers upon the facticity attributed to them apart from the whole fabric of human experience. Religion viewed as a collection of beliefs and behaviors or maturity portrayed as a generic term for what is defined as socially acceptable, do not need to be integrated with lived-experience. Add, however, the descriptor "spiritual" to maturity and a wholly different concept begins to emerge, one which sheds the constraints imposed both by "religion" and "maturity."

When the idea of what constitutes the spiritual is combined with an understanding of maturity that reaches beyond its popular meanings, we have a synergistic concept which produces a dynamic way of describing a person open to wrestling with issues of ultimacy, a person willing to risk transcending both the relativities of religious beliefs and behaviors and also socio-cultural expectations about maturity, a person ready

> to confront the boundaries of life and death, to grapple with hope and despair, to puzzle over decisions of good, evil, and mixtures of both . . . to [walk] to the edges of mystery at the heart of existence.[5]

This passage from Eugene Bianchi's book, *Aging as a Spiritual Journey*, illustrates the faith which undergirds spiritual maturity. Faith is here taken to be the active way in which the ego synthesizes meaning related to the self, others, the world and the transcendent. Faith understood like this is an active process rather than a static dogma possessed by institutions and imposed upon persons. As James Fowler writes, faith is the "dynamic patterned process by which we find life meaningful."[6]

The work of Fowler on faith development and of Erikson on the psychological strengths available in old age point us toward a deeper theoretical appreciation of the spiritual maturity expressed by elders whose trust, hope, and even faith may be severely tested by the panoply of changes, losses and suffering which so often accompany the aging process. How does the elder continue to find life meaningful when a foot must be amputated, when a life-long friend dies, when a spouse's personality becomes ravaged by Alzheimer's disease, when a beloved home must be sold, when one receives attention only because of "problems" others believe they must solve?

For some, the experiences of aging produce bitterness, despair, self-centeredness, suspicion — in short, all the negative characteristics attributed to the aged since Aristotle. Others do not dwell upon the travails of the present; they make their peace with the triumphs and defeats of the past. Free from envy, they find themselves able to care about persons of other generations. Knowing the limits of their own lives, they demonstrate genuine concern about securing a safer world for the future. They differ from those who have been unable or unwilling to overcome their narcissistic fantasies of completely separating the "good" from the "bad" and who find in aging only frustration, bitterness, and despair. Those individuals who have come to the latter years of their lives with a measure of trust, hope and faith consciously acknowledge the paradoxes of aging and are rewarded with a sense of wholeness or integration.

The ongoing psychological growth of these persons has allowed them to claim the trait of ego integrity; they possess a sense of "coherence and wholeness"[7] to which they can appeal when tested by the sufferings of their own particular lives. Further, their faith has become "conjunctive"; they can tolerate the ambiguities of their own experience and they can creatively cope with the tensions of paradox.[8]

Nonetheless, although these individuals recognize that their integrity opens them to the realm of the whole, they remain aware that their understanding is partial. Spiritual maturity, which embraces the psychological condition of ego integrity and the faith which Fowler calls "conjunctive," requires humility. Further, persons who fit this description offer vivid reminders of the fact that spiritual maturity grants no reprieve from the changes, losses and suffering of aging. Instead, spiritual maturity represents a profound sense of trust and hope that meaning and order endure despite threats of meaningless and disorder. This trust and hope are not centered in the self nor in other persons nor in the world of places and things. All these are understood to be ephemeral and full of ambiguity and contradiction. Rather, trust and hope are centered in the transcendent realm, the realm of mystery, but also, finally, of certainty.

Given all this, how can we suggest that humor is an expression of spiritual maturity? As will be demonstrated in the next section, humor can be an expression of trust, hope and even faith. It represents one way spiritually mature persons respond to the paradoxes and particularities of age with an overriding sense of wholeness and integration.

UNDERSTANDING HUMOR AS AN EXPRESSION OF SPIRITUAL MATURITY

Of the many theories and interpretations of humor, the psychoanalytic approach comes the closest to being able to explain how humor enables people to achieve a sense of wholeness in spite of experiences of particularity. Sigmund Freud believed that humor enables the ego to obtain pleasure from a situation expected to produce unpleasure. It

> comes about . . . at the cost of an affect that does not occur: it arises from an economy in the expenditure of affect.[9]

To Freud, the many kinds of humor vary according to which emotion is economized, be it fear or horror, pity or sadness, anger or despair. For example, humor permits aging persons to encounter physical, social and psychological traumas with an unexpected response: laughter. The individual who makes a humorous remark about the aging body economizes on the affect of self-pity but at the same time does not avoid recognition of physical difficulties by denying, rationalizing or even repressing their existence.

Freud called the pleasure of humor "liberating and elevating."[10] He said that humor possesses a kind of grandeur, and he used words like "triumph" and "victory" to describe it. Yet, one suspects that he would not have used these words if laughter was constant and humor was the only response made to human experience.

Freud recognized in his paper, "On Transience," that what is fleeting is also precious.[11] The individual who can never be serious, who treats all of life's misfortunes as cause for joking, does not experience the liberation of humor but rather becomes imprisoned by it, unable authentically to experience other, nonhumorous, responses. Heinz Kohut, describing the person "unable to be serious who employs humor excessively," observed that the ego in that case has been unable and unwilling to recognize "those unalterable realities which oppose the assertions of the narcissistic self."[12] In other words, the person who cannot accept suffering cannot also experience the liberation from suffering which humor grants. Thus, Freud's work on mourning and loss and his work on humor can be seen as complementary. In his work on mourning, he wrote that the ego suffers terribly at the loss of a beloved object.[13] Kohut similarly wrote of the suffering experienced when the ego accepts the limitations of its narcissism and thus transforms that narcissism. The endurance of that suffering forges the perspective necessary for an authentic humor, which, as Freud said, "surmounts the automatism of defense."[14]

The perspective of humor, which enables persons to transcend the tensions of paradox, is itself paradoxical. It requires a kind of detachment, a self-transcendence, and at the same time demands an intimacy with events, other persons and the self. Laughter and smiling, the physical responses to humor, indicate that the perspective of humor, the "standing back," necessary to generate the humor is paradoxically associated with an utter immersion in the experience.

Perhaps an example of this perspective would be helpful at this point. Once an old woman lay dying in a hospital bed when her pastor came to call on her. In the course of their conversation, he told her a story about St. Francis who one day was hoeing his gar-

den. A stranger passed and asked St. Francis what he would do if he
knew the world was going to end in the next hour. St. Francis replied that he would change nothing and continue to hoe his garden.
The pastor telling this story reflected on how much at peace with
himself and the world St. Francis was and he was startled when his
listener, much encumbered by tubes and needles and bandages, began to laugh heartily. In response to his question of why she
laughed, she replied, "He wouldn't, and I couldn't!"

Authentic humor triumphs over suffering when suffering has
been consciously acknowledged. Authentic humor does not, however, create suffering. Here lies the ethical dimension of any discussion of humor. Some humor is "morally inappropriate" as philosopher John Morreall put it.[15] Likewise, Conrad Hyers, taking a cue
from Aristotle's differentiation of liberal and illiberal laughter,
noted the moral responsibility inherent in the freedom laughter provides.[16]

The humor which takes seriously the moral responsibility of its
freedom is authentic humor. The ego capable of this type of humor
must have acknowledged suffering and must know that suffering
cannot be evaded or denied through laughter. Rather, the humor
which represents, as Kohut would say, a transformation of narcissism, bursts through suffering, provides a perspective on it, and
momentarily relieves its pain. Because the ego has accepted limitations on its narcissism, it includes itself in the humorous perspective
and does not use humor to proclaim itself invulnerable to the things
which make another person's actions laughable. In Erik Erikson's
words, it is wholistic and not totalistic; it includes and does not
exclude.[17]

In its inclusiveness, the authentic humor of the spiritually mature
person conveys a profound sense of trust and of hope. To be able to
adopt a humorous attitude toward the ludicrous and the incongruous
aspects of human existence rather than denying or repressing them,
demonstrates a sense of trust which detects wholeness underlying
particularity. To perceive incongruity and laugh rather than despair
points to a trust in a higher order of meaning which unifies the
divided. Or, as philosopher Marie Collins Swabey wrote, in humor,
"we detect an incongruence as cancelled by an underlying congru-

ence." She went on to say that "we gain an inkling, as it were, of the hang of things, sometimes even a hint of cosmic beneficence."[18]

Because aging persons who have achieved a sense of spiritual maturity continue to feel a deep, almost visceral sense of trust in a universe shaped by order and meaning, they can laugh without fear that their laughter will shatter their world like a hammer blow shatters glass. In aging persons, authentic humor states, "You have done something silly but I have done silly things, too. In our laughter, let us celebrate our oneness." And humor says, "I am old and slow yet burning with life. Let our laughter together celebrate our trust in an order which transcends age and its ills." Trusting in coherence which overcomes incoherence, meaning which underlies frustration, wholeness which transcends particularity, the aging person open to the humorous attitude expresses a sense of hopefulness.

Conrad Hyers has written about the relation between humor and hope in a way which applies well to the challenges faced by aging people. Humor he says,

> may express a certain heroic defiance in the face of life's most crushing defeats, an unquenchable nobility of spirit that refuses to permit a given fate or oppressor to have the last word — to be absolute. The human spirit has not been utterly vanquished. The will to live and the determination to continue the struggle, or the faith that the struggle will be continued, has not been finally conquered. Where there is humor, there is still hope.[19]

USING HUMOR TO PROMOTE SPIRITUAL MATURITY

Florida Scott-Maxwell wrote that life without laughter was "inhuman." In seeking laughter, she sought not merely the physical act of laughing (which can be feigned and triggered by numerous situations unrelated to humor) but rather laughter in response to humor. Humor, as Conrad Hyers notes, "is an important part of what it means to be human and humane."[20] It offers perspective, but this is not a totally detached type of perspective which views life from a remote location untouched by suffering. Authentic humor triumphs over suffering by first acknowledging that suffering. While humor permits a distancing from that which causes suffering and conflict and confusion, at the same time it represents an intimacy with the paradoxes of human life and culture which cause that pain.

Understanding this, we can begin to conceive of ways that persons who offer various forms of care to elders can use humor to promote or reinforce the sense of spiritual maturity. Authentic humor reaches out and draws others into its aura of delight; it unites persons across what might initially appear to be vast psychosocial distances. Doubtless many of the physicians, psychotherapists, religious workers and others whose work includes contacts with aging persons already have a strong intuitive sense of the healing ways of humor. Sometimes, however, we may not fully comprehend how authentic humor can be an expression of the spiritual dimension. Believing that spiritual maturity is only expressed through the "eternal verities," we may devalue humor.

For example, we might imagine a young doctor who approaches the bedside of a chronically ill elder. Should the doctor interpret the elder's attempts at humor as defensive resistance to medical "facts"? Or, should this physician attempt to comprehend the deep spiritual reserves which offer this individual the triumph of laughter in the face of death's approach? The physician herself might even initiate a humorous exchange with the patient, not in any way that demeans that person's suffering, but so as to affirm the essential humanity which they share, however different their circumstances might be.[21]

Psychotherapists also can employ authentic humor to enable their clients to reach a new perspective on themselves. Recognizing the caution with which they must use and interpret humor in therapy, those therapists open to the spiritual dimensions of their clients' travails ought to be able to recognize the ways humor promotes growth; it can facilitate a person's approach to the issues which must be resolved so that spiritual maturity might be attained.[22]

Finally, religious workers should understand that humor can be a valuable resource available to support their goals of promoting and sustaining spiritual maturity in elders. Humor and the faith of the spiritually mature need not be seen as contradictory. The humor which enables a person to laugh in spite of suffering is an articulation of faith in an ultimate order which heals brokenness. Humor without faith, on the other hand, expresses despair and bitterness; it is inauthentic and must be recognized as such. Through a deeper appreciation of humor, religious workers might achieve a more complete understanding of the spiritual well-being of the aging persons they encounter. Also, through humor, they might even be able to gain important insights into the spirituality of persons afflicted by neurological impairments.

Physicians, psychotherapists and, in particular, religious workers need to recognize that humor alone is not the only way that spiritual maturity can be articulated. But, because it enables persons to overcome the tensions of paradox while maintaining trust, hope and faith, humor represents a significant expression of the way aging people of spiritual maturity reach out to embrace wholeness.

NOTES

1. Erik Erikson, *Young Man Luther* (New York: W. W. Norton, 1958), p. 51.

2. Florida Scott-Maxwell, *The Measure of My Days* (New York: A. A. Knopf, 1968), p. 8.

3. For another interpretation of religious maturity, see S. H. McFadden, "Attributes of Religious Maturity in Aging People," *Journal of Religion and Aging*, 1 (1985):39-48.

4. Richard Coan, *Hero, Artist, Sage or Saint?* (New York: Columbia University Press, 1977), pp. 74-75.

5. Eugene Bianchi, *Aging as a Spiritual Journey* (New York: Crossroad, 1982), p. 177.

6. James Fowler, *Stages of Faith* (New York: Harper & Row, 1981), p. 8.

7. Erik Erikson, *The Life Cycle Completed* (New York: W. W. Norton, 1982), p. 65.

8. Fowler, pp. 197-198.

9. Sigmund Freud, *Jokes and Their Relation to the Unconscious*, in *Standard Edition*, vol. 8, ed. and trans. James Strachey (London: Hogarth Press, 1960), p. 228.

10. Sigmund Freud, "Humor," in *Standard Edition*, vol. 21, ed. and trans. James Strachey (London: Hogarth Press, 1961), p. 166.

11. Sigmund Freud, "On Transience," in *Standard Edition*, vol. 21, ed. and trans. James Strachey (London: Hogarth Press, 1957).

12. Heinz Kohut, "Forms and Transformations of Narcissism," *Journal of the American Psychoanalytic Association*, 14 (1966):267.

13. Sigmund Freud, "Mourning and Melancholia," in *Standard Edition*, vol. 14, ed. and trans. James Strachey (London: Hogarth Press, 1957).

14. Freud, *Jokes*, p. 233.

15. John Morreall, *Taking Laughter Seriously* (Albany, NY: State University of New York Press, 1983), p. 110.

16. Conrad Hyers, *The Comic Vision and the Christian Faith* (New York: Pilgrim Press, 1981), pp. 27-28.

17. For Erikson's differentiation of wholism from totalism, see Erik Erikson, *Identity: Youth and Crisis* (New York: W. W. Norton, 1968), pp. 80-90.

18. Marie Collins Swabey, *Comic Laughter: A Philosophic Essay* (New Haven: Yale University Press, 1961), p. v.

19. Hyers, p. 36.

20. Ibid., p. 11.

21. The literature on the relation between humor and health is growing. See, for example, Vera Robinson, "Humor and Health," in *Handbook of Humor Research*, vol. II, ed. P. E. McGhee and J. H. Goldstein (New York: Springer-Verlag, 1983), pp. 109-128. Also, see H. M. Lefcourt and R. A. Martin, *Humor and Life Stress* (New York: Springer-Verlag, 1986).

22. For a collection of papers on humor and psychotherapy, see A. J. Chapman and H. C. Foot, *It's a Funny Thing, Humor* (New York: Pergamon Press, 1977).

Christian Perspectives
on Spiritual Needs of a Human Being

Leo E. Missinne, PhD

SUMMARY. Each human being, independent of culture, time, and age has three fundamental needs. A need for biophysical exchanges, a need for psychosocial exchanges, and a need for spiritual-integrated exchanges. Spiritual needs are not separated from biological, social, psychological, and material aspects of life. Christian spirituality today is oriented toward responding to life, to its beauty and injustices, to the universe, and is responsive and responsible to the poor. Some specific tasks for older people today are commitment to the great causes of justice, peace, and environmental protection, and a deeper bond of love for God and fellow man.

INTRODUCTION

Understanding and explaining human behavior is not an easy task. Nothing is as complicated as the behavior of human beings because of the mixed influences of heredity, environment, will, and other elements we can barely give names to. Some people are very simplistic in talking about human behavior. Jung critiqued this shallow approach:

> I am aware that most people believe they know all there is to be known about psychology because they think that psychology is nothing but what they know of themselves.[1]

It seems to me that there is first of all a distinction to make between understanding and explaining behavior. Sometimes we understand why a person behaves in a particular way, but we cannot

Leo E. Missinne is Professor of Gerontology, University of Nebraska at Omaha, Omaha, NE 68182.

explain it. On the other hand we may be able to explain a certain behavior, but we cannot understand how or why that person did it. Understanding has a more emotional undertone. Explaining has a more intellectual or rational basis. Both are necessary when studying human behavior.

There are some aspects of behavior that can only be understood through intuitions and sensations, through a kind of spiritual experience in which one is directly united with the "other." Too often we avoid using this important method because such an approach would be dangerous, or will jeopardize the validity of our interpretation of his or her behavior. We lose a great deal through these fears, which force us to make judgments based only on our intellectual observation.

I. BASIC HUMAN NEEDS

Many psychologists explain human behavior as attempts to fulfill a need. This need may be conscious or unconscious. The emphasis of many psychological theories on *one* fundamental force or need as an explanation of human behavior has influenced psychological theories in general and has resulted in many distorted explanations of behavior in daily life. We may be able to identify a basic need in a human being which seems to act as the origin of a particular behavior, but that does not mean that this need is the *only* one. Sometimes one need is more dominant in a particular society, in a particular time, or in a particular person. For example, the sexual need may have been a more dominant and by the same token a more repressed and frustrated need in a Victorian culture. Freud's personality and his theory can only be understood in the framework of his time and the particular culture which existed at the beginning of the nineteenth century.

We can say that a "Number One" mentality is evident in all aspects of life in the American culture of today. People feel "no good" if they cannot win, if they are only "Number Two." Such behavior has its roots in the need for power, to be the best, to be important, to assert oneself, and to be admired. This need, which did not exist as much, for example, in the Middle Ages in Europe, or in some African cultures, could be the origin of all kinds of behaviors, and may be helpful in understanding and explaining behavior.

Similarly, the need for purpose, the search for meaning of life as a basic need was very strongly accentuated in Europe after World War II, under the influence of the school of Existentialism, the philosophy of Sartre, Heidegger, and Kierkegaard. This need was expressed powerfully in the literature of that time and discussed intensely in daily conversations. The atmosphere of war time and the Holocaust was such a unique experience of repression and of the frustrations of the need to find meaning, that it gave that need an importance it does not completely deserve.

Trying to explain *all* human behavior in terms of sexuality, the search for power, or the need for meaning is going too far. These labels fit certain people in certain cultures or in a particular time in their life, but they are certainly not the only drive or need for every human being at all times.

It seems to me that there are three basic needs which each human being has, old or young, black or white, African or Asian, European or American.[2] These three needs are not in a hierarchical order. The distinction of these needs does not mean that they are separated from each other. They are interrelated in different degrees and forms of human behaviors. I believe there is in each human being:

a. a need for biophysical exchange;
b. a need for psychosocial exchange; and
c. a need for spiritual integrated exchange.

A. The Need for Biophysical Exchange

Human beings must be in contact, must exchange with the physical environment in order to live and be themselves. We need air, food, drink, warmth, etc. . . . . Too much or too little of this biophysical exchange creates problems and endangers our chances of being ourselves. For example, we are not able to be ourselves if we eat or drink too much, if we eat or drink too little, if we are too tired or too cold. Everyone has to know his/her own measure in fulfilling these needs, which will vary with time, age, culture, and circumstances.

People like to touch and to be touched, so they know that they are not alone. This physical touch may be expressed by encountering the eyes of the other, hugging or touching. To experience the bio-physical presence of the other will help us to be more ourselves and to trust the feeling that we exist. For example, people in danger will congregate, just to feel the presence of one another. Persons isolated from other human beings and nature cannot be themselves and act normally. This biophysical exchange is essential for people to be themselves, and to have confidence in themselves.

B. The Need for Psychosocial Exchange

At every moment of our life we are building and nourishing our personality in and through psychosocial contact with other people. Every person wants to maintain and to develop her/himself on a psychosocial level. If we feel ignored or neglected by others, it is felt as a loss to our personal existence. We have the impression that we are less ourselves. We need others in order to communicate, to refine our thoughts and to receive new information.

The best way to express this need is in Eric Fromm's formula that *love and work* is the essence of what human life is all about.[3] In order to be ourselves we must be able to love others and to know that we are loved. We must be able to work for others and we must know that other people are working for us. To "love and to work" are two of the most important manifestations of this fundamental need for psychosocial exchange. Giving oneself to others through love and work is a form of contact and development for which every person feels a need, because it is by giving that we keep ourselves psychosocially alive. It is by feeling loved that we acquire confidence in ourselves to create and to give ourselves more to others. This need for psychosocial contact through love and work is important not only for young people but for older people as well, and is important in every stage of human development.

If people cannot work or are not allowed to work, because of sickness or a handicap, they must be able to replace their work life with a degree of love — to love more and to become more lovable in order to be human. That is one of the reasons why younger people have not only to learn to work, but more important why they have to learn to love and to make themselves lovable in order to be prepared for their older days, for the days when they can no longer work because of illness or in becoming handicapped. If we cannot replace the lost capability of being able to work through more love, it will create a real disaster in our life, and an obstacle to being ourselves.

C. The Need for Spiritual Integrated Exchange

Insofar as we are not completely absorbed in our psychosocial and biophysical exchanges, we experience the need to maintain and to illuminate ourselves beyond our existence. We like to know our place in the universe, and the meaning of our own existence. We like to have some answers to questions about and beyond our own existence. Religions and spiritual manifestations provide the most striking examples of the need to maintain and to illuminate human existence through an interaction and exchange that goes beyond biophysical and psychosocial facts. This need can be expressed in a form of a request for support from the absolute, it can be found in a desire to be at peace with one's conscience or with God. "Saving one's soul" or being a "link in a chain of evolution" are other expressions which indicate this need for spiritual integrated exchange, and living beyond our own earthly life.

This same need is apparent in the natural tendency profoundly rooted in human beings of being able to survive their own life in and through their children or through their creations and achievements. It appears in the joy of the grandfather who holds on to life by waiting for the birth or the graduation of a grandson or granddaughter. It can be found in the need of an instructor who loves to educate more and more disciples in order to prolong the life of his/her own ideas and discoveries. We need to know and to feel ourselves spiritually integrated beyond our own existence into an absolute order of existence, which will help us to be more ourselves and to unfold our existence into the global universe.

II. REFLECTIONS ON SPIRITUAL NEEDS

The term "spiritual" is a very complex term. There are several aspects within this term, which have to be distinguished.

a. The spiritual is a dimension which cannot be separated from biological, psychological, social, material, and other aspects of life. Johnson addresses this idea by saying:

> We have seen that the definition of "spiritual" is not so clear and rigidly fixed that it can be separated from the physical, psychological, material, and other aspects of human existence. Instead it is a component or dimension of man which runs through all of the person and his behavior, providing an orientation and focus which pertains to all of the positively valued joys and experiences of living and all of the negative problems and fears of life and death. It provides a basis for coping with the disruptions of removal (mobility of children and grandchildren, death of spouse and friends, moving away from the old neighborhood), of biological insecurity (illness, death, and disrupted sexual functioning), and of sinfulness and its feelings of guilt.[4]

Life *is* interaction. An interplay of different parts. No part can live just by itself. Our spiritual needs are connected with and influence the psychosocial and biophysical needs of our life. It is difficult to have healthy children who will prolong your life if you are sick or poor or are not able to love and to be loved. In our Western approach toward reality, we like to make rational and clear distinctions of entities. In fact, we are inclined to divide and to make dualistic approaches to everything we see and experience, and we forget that we also sometimes kill the reality by dividing and separating. We divide things and phenomena into opposites: body and soul, male and female, black and white, Democrats and Republicans, Christians and pagans, day and night, spiritual and material, etc. Such an attitude does not exist in many other cultures. For example, some traditional African peoples make no distinction between the spiritual and the other aspects of life. Everything is spiritual. An African takes his spiritual explanations to his work, to his harvest, to his family life, to his success and suffering. If the harvest was not good it's because God, or the ancestors, or the spirits did not bless the harvest and is punishing the individual for some bad actions.

b. The term "spiritual" is a broader term than "religious." Spiritual is connected with things beyond all material phenomena. Listening to music, reading or writing good literature, to know and to understand, to enjoy a sunset, to paint and to admire a painting, to pray and to meditate, to sing, to love and be loved, all these different rational and emotional experiences are a part of our spiritual life. They not only give us joy and bring us in contact with beauty but they also are bases for coping with losses, with failures, with suffering and death. The term religious is geared toward describing individual or group relations with a supernatural power, whether called God, or spirits or vital force. Etymologically, the word religion comes from the Latin word "re-ligare," which means to "bind together with." Human beings as a group, or the individual and, in fact, creation as a whole, have to bind themselves together with the source of all existence. This would indicate that religion as a common or an individual approach to being "together with God or spirits" is a relationship beyond ourselves and beyond the boundaries of a community.

c. The relationship between "religion and spiritual" is not always a positive one, just as relations between certain paintings, certain kinds of music, certain kinds of love are not always ones of joy and spiritual growth. Sometimes religion can harm or destroy spiritual life and spiritual growth. For example, Jesus criticized some Pharisees for obeying the letter of the law and not the spirit. "They honor me with lip service, but their heart is far from me," he said. Observing only the letter of the law in our religious practices can kill our spiritual life, and our relations with God, nature and beauty.

d. The term "spiritual" signifies both one's search for the meaning of life in general, and for meaning in the many events of daily life, which we could call "provisional meanings." Provisional meanings are in fact "glimpses" of the ultimate meaning of our life.[5] Working on a project, having some ideals to realize, a sudden awareness of beauty, a momentary sense of deep inner peace, an experience of longing for beauty and love or a positive attitude in suffering, are all provisional meanings which will help us to find our ultimate meaning in life. The search for meaning is an expression of the spiritual dimension of each human being, and separates us from the animal world. Human beings don't just exist. They are asking questions about their existence, which is a typical spiritual aspect of being human.[6]

III. TRENDS IN TODAY'S CHRISTIAN SPIRITUALITY

The trends in today's Christian spirituality are evidenced in literature and in Christian behavior. They are different from the trends expressed in other times. It seems to me that in the present time there are four fundamental trends to be distinguished:

a. Christian spirituality responds to life, to its beauty and its injustices, and leads to action. This response is reflected in a person's prayers. Prayer is a response to life, which takes place in enjoyment of beauty through mysticism, or which becomes a source of courage in fighting the injustices in the world. Prayer is no longer as it was centuries ago, a withdrawal from the world. Prayer today realizes the union with God through beauty or through the cry for justice. This union with God will invite Christians to be sensitive to all aspects of life, the psychosocial as well as a physiological ones — human rights and hunger, generosity, and freedom.

b. Christian spirituality today looks to the universe. The whole world becomes a part of a Christian personality. People who suffer in India, in Africa, or in Central America as well as our own neighbors, are becoming a part of the world of a Christian. The center of prayer and action is not just personal needs or the needs of our inner circle but the needs of all human beings, especially the poorest and the most needy in whatever place or culture they may be living. This trend is a consequence of a modern world dominated by the power of media and telecommunications which brings us into direct contact with the universe.

c. Christian spirituality today is responsive and responsible to the poor and oppressed. By listening to the poor, people are listening to God. This is the theme of liberation theologians. Authentic Christian spiritual life suggests that the oppressed are not just recipients of prayers of charity, but they have a significant voice in the interpretation of the gospel. The poor have been the first recipients of Christ's doctrine and the first proclaimers of the gospel. By listening to what the poor have to tell us, we are listening to Christ and his message.

d. Christian spirituality today is social oriented. Not only the persons, but also the society in which a person is living is important in a relationship with God. God relates not only to individuals but also to groups, social entities. Through the events or aspects of a society in which people live, God invites us to realize good things for other human beings. God is an inviting God. God invites us to act but does not force us. We enjoy the freedom to follow the invitation or not.

CONCLUSION

Christian spirituality today is each person's particular expression of these spiritual integrated needs. These expressions can materialize for older adults in many important tasks that give meaning to their life and help them to be more themselves. Some of these include: (1) a commitment to the great causes of justice, peace, and environmental protection, (2) a deeper bond of love and service for God and fellow human beings; and (3) a new interior growth of spiritual life through faith, hope, and love.

Through such an approach older adults will not only self-actualize but they will transcend themselves for greater causes. This self-transcendence will lead them out of their ego-centered existence and help them to do something for the generations to come, that nature may be preserved, that justice may triumph, that the oppression of sexism, racism, ethnocentrism may end and people may love each other and God.

Through such actions older adults will be able to fulfill in a special way this spiritual integrated exchange need. This specific way of transcending themselves could be the beginning of a new life in God after their life here on earth.

NOTES

1. Carl G. Jung, *Psychology and Religion: West and East* (Princeton, N.J.: Princeton University Press, 1959), p. 470.

2. Many of the ideas concerning the three basic needs are inspired by lectures of Dr. Joseph Muttin at the University of Louvain in 1955-57. They can be found in his book *Psychoanalysis and Personality* (New York: New American Library, 1962).

3. Eric Fromm, *The Art of Loving* (New York: Perennial Publishers, 1974).

4. Gerald K. Johnson, "Spiritual Aspects of Aging," *Lutheran Social Welfare Quarterly*, 4 (1964): 28-36.

5. Leo E. Missinne and Judy Willeke-Kay, "Reflections on the Meaning of Life in Older Age," *Journal of Religion and Aging*, 1 (Summer 1985): 47-48.

6. Viktor E. Frankl, *The Doctor and the Soul* (New York: A. A. Knopf, 1965), pp. IX-X.

Countering Cultural Metaphors of Aging

Henry C. Simmons, PhD

SUMMARY. This article examines three clusters of metaphors or cultural images of aging which function to marginalize older adults: metaphors which focus on aging as physical decline, on aging as aesthetic distance from youth, and on aging as failure of productivity. It then sketches out two ways to counter the marginalizing power of these cultural images of aging, to shape new metaphors or images of aging within a community of meaning, and to help make new sense of growing old, namely the formation of face-to-face groups of older adults and the creation of rituals in worship which name publicly the realities and experiences of aging.

When we speak about life's biggest issues—life itself, death, God, reality, human nature, growing old—we use images and metaphors to help us name the unnameable. These images and metaphors are more than simple designations. They are words and phrases which convey knowledge, which tend to action, and which evoke feeling and emotion. They tell us, interactively, what we can know, what we should do, and even what we should feel. The metaphors and images we use to speak about the great realities of life enmesh us in our culture's instructions about the meaning of these realities. They are "the web which binds us each to the other, and all to the life of which we are an inseparable part—binds us to the invisible shapes that have gone and those to come in the solidarity of one flowing whole."[1]

The interaction of Church and Synagogue with those who grow old occurs in a context of cultural values, metaphors, and images of aging which shape this interaction and response. I address three

---

Henry C. Simmons is Professor, Presbyterian School of Christian Education, 1205 Palmyra Avenue, Richmond, VA 23227.

clusters of popular metaphors and images of aging, each of which has some truth and much power, but each of which is at root inadequate and inappropriate. These metaphors marginalize, that is they remove the aging person from the center of what is authentically human. These are aging as physical decline, aging as aesthetic distance from youth, and aging as failure of productivity. Clearly these metaphors function differently for men and women, for middle-class and working-class, for white and black, anglo and hispanic, for those who were born in 1900 and those who were born in 1925. This article is written by a middle-class white male, born in 1938, of Canadian citizenship, living in Richmond, Virginia, whose primary attention has been focused on middle-class whites born quite early in this century.

AGING AS PHYSICAL DECLINE

Frequently our culture portrays older adults as tottering, forgetful, slow-witted and helpless—images which focus on physical decline. Even some apparently more benign metaphors we use for these years, for example "golden age," "sunset years," or even Dr. Seuss' playful "obsolete children," cast our understanding of, our response to, and our feeling about aging within the framework of physical decline. Of course, even the healthiest old age will end in death, and many people do suffer physical decline as they grow older, but this does not explain why we *focus* on metaphors of physical decline when we try to understand aging. People grow old and weak in other cultures, some of which do not structure their understanding of aging in terms of physical decline, even though they recognize the distinctive nature of final frailty.

There is a very substantial literature on the physiology of aging; research in medicine and cell biology is a well-developed aspect of gerontology, and this may color our perception of what it means to grow older. Physics in our culture is "hard science"; the rest, including the human, is "soft." The world of physics is objective; other worlds are somehow tainted by subjectivity. This stands in complex contrast to any religious world-view which describes God as spirit.

A focus on physical decline does not imply a recognition of

death. What we see ritualized in mortuary and funeral practices is evidence of a culture which hides away from death. Our culture teaches us to think of death as if it were an option.

We may catch glimpses of how much metaphors of aging as physical decline affect our own thinking about aging, our responses to older adults, and our feelings and fears about our own later years. Some evidence that this metaphor may be internalized less powerfully by white women than by white males is found in the disproportionately high suicide rate for white males over 80 years of age.

AGING AS AESTHETIC DISTANCE FROM YOUTH

There is another group of metaphors and images (over-the-hill, crone, washed up, dirty old man) which casts aging in the context of aesthetic distance from youth, with youth understood as the time of life which is the most desirable, most sought after, most normative for what is human. This metaphor highlights the aesthetic and visual differences between the old and the young, and recognizes the young as normatively beautiful. This cult of youth has been furthered by sophisticated industries which cater both to the demands of youth and the need of the rest to imitate youth.

Age viewed as aesthetic distance from youth affects the middle-aged particularly. Children or adolescents may fervently hope that life will get better when they are grownups, although they do not imagine that when they are grownup they will also be getting closer to old age. The old often experience sadness when they see their reflection in the mirror because the face they see is not the self they experience. But it is the middle-aged who understand in their guts the terrors of moving away from youth. As Ronald Blythe puts it:

> The middle-aged frequently find themselves — timidly yet compulsively, like tonguing a tooth nerve — measuring their assets against those of old age to see what has to go. It is often a great deal in both cases. There can be then a spiritual and physical drawing back from the old, as if they possessed some centrifugal force to drag the no longer young into their slipstream decay.[2]

Aesthetic distance from youth functions differently as a cultural metaphor for men and women. An 80-year-old man can still be handsome, but it is unlikely that an 80-year-old woman will be perceived as beautiful (even if we see that she once was beautiful) although the man's and woman's faces may be equally wrinkled. Why? It has been suggested from the world of the stage that, aesthetically, wrinkles cast shadows and therefore create ambiguity. Thus the question shifts to ask why the culture allows the old man and not the woman to be ambiguous. It may be that our public morality expects the male who faced the dangers and opportunities of the marketplace to be ambiguous while the woman who was charged with preserving virtue and morality is not.[3] "We were never free," a woman writes, "even to use those four-letter words we all know, because the chief duty of females, we were taught, was to practice the restraints of civilization, not explore its possibilities."[4]

This analysis, if it is correct, gives us a glimpse of the ways in which cultural images and metaphors of aging affect thinking, response, and feeling in a mysterious amalgam. It also highlights the androcentric nature of our culture. Women are marginalized differently from men because women do not begin at the center of the circle of power. Men, too, will eventually lose power, although this may more likely occur through physical decline. In either case this marginalization sets up a powerful internal threat.

AGING AS FAILURE OF PRODUCTIVITY

There is yet another group of metaphors which stress failure of productivity: retired persons, has-beens—words that define the self in terms of previous employment. Americans are a pragmatic and a functional people who tend to identify themselves with their doing rather than with their being. To the extent that "person as producer" is a dominant image of life, the cessation of productive employment is an understandable if potentially pernicious metaphor for aging.

Those who have been relatively successful as producers are likely to find, according to recent research, that retirement "usually has little or no negative effects on health, activities, and attitudes and retirement reduces income on average by only about one-fourth."[5] How does this square with the more common wisdom about loss of identity through cessation of work? "When retirement strips them of their work, people forfeit their identity. They lose their self-respect and therefore their hold on the respect of others. The aged slip to the margins of consciousness for the ruling generation."[6]

Two possible explanations suggest themselves: (1) the more financially successful may still perceive a strong sense of identity through their working capital. Although the capitalist spirit would strongly discourage the enjoyment of the fruits of earlier success, those who have working capital with which they are identified and which is intrinsic to their sense of self may describe themselves as retired although in fact they perceive themselves still to be working. (2) Quite a different (although not mutually exclusive) explanation comes from observation of the self-indulgent, almost narcissistic lifestyles of some retired people. One wonders whether this is escapist behavior cloaking a loss of self. Were that the case, there would be reason to mistrust the self-reports of retirement as a basically satisfying time of life, or at least to see the early part of retirement — before the diminishments of age — as an extension of middle age.

Metaphors of aging as failure of productivity may be ambiguous. But there seems no question that our culture uses these metaphors as one powerful explanation of the meaning of aging and of appropriate response in action and affect. Such metaphors remind us of the integrality of work to life. They also serve to remind us of the cumulative injuries of social class: people who have lived on the edges of the economy without any security and with little continuity of employment have known work as a brutal reality, not as productive in a personal sense.

COUNTERING THE CULTURE'S METAPHORS

As avowedly religious people, we expect — at least if we read seriously the documents of our various religious communities — that we have insights, actions, and values to contribute to aging. Indeed we offer interpretive schemas or systems of meaning which seek and claim to offer meaning in face of the great questions of life:

meaning, integrity, isolation or community, death. These interpretive schemas are cast in language which stands alongside and competes with the "language used in everyday life [which] continuously provides me with the necessary objectifications and posits the order within which these make sense and within which everyday life has meaning for me."'

To the extent that we are faithful to our religious traditions, our interpretations will not simply be those of the prevailing culture. Our metaphors will in some way be counter cultural. I believe it is possible, although very difficult, for Church or Synagogue to break the power of the culture's images which form the meaning of aging. But if we are to attend seriously to this problem, we must be aware of its centrality in the life of people as they grow old.

THE CENTRALITY OF THE PROBLEM

In the last fifty years or so there has been an increasing emphasis on the responsibility of Church and Synagogue to provide care for the vulnerable old, in direct service, in provision of funds, and in the mobilization of volunteers. This emphasis is often capsulized in the phrase "ministry *to* the aging." More recently there has been an emphasis on engaging the older adult as a productive member of the community. This emphasis is noted in the phrase "ministry *with* the aging." As necessary as these may be, they must not distract us from the most pressing and urgent needs which religion has always tried to address — and which are even more urgent as one ages: namely how to live with integrity, in relationship with others, and how to make sense of life and death in face of diminishment and the threat of personal annihilation. It may be argued that to focus on these problems to the detriment of feeding the hungry, housing the homeless, or caring for the sick perverts something at the heart of religion. But these actions must be accomplished in a way that constantly reaffirms the full humanity of those who need care. If a person is fed, and clothed, and housed — and knows himself or herself to be increasingly less and less a person — an even more fundamental harm is done. And this will inevitably be the case to the extent that culture's metaphors by which aging is understood remain unchallenged.

BREAKING LOOSE FROM MARGINAL TO LIMINAL

It is not an easy task to break loose from the images of one's own culture. "It takes severe biographical shocks to disintegrate the massive reality internalized in early childhood"[8] and proportionally severe biographic jolts or their equivalents to even recognize the images and metaphors which have power over us. But it is possible. What we notice in common with the three clusters of metaphors of which I have spoken is that they all make the older adult marginal. They all make the older adult to be seen by self or others as increasingly further from the center of reality, from the point of normative humanity. The movement away from the center—a movement which is all the more difficult the more satisfied a person is with the view from the center!—is initiated subtly at first and then increasingly brutally by the culture. It is so difficult to resist because all the participants have internalized the same set of rules: to be human is to be young and strong and productive. However, it may be that to be marginal has its own possibilities for challenges to prevailing cultural instructions.

In his study of rites of passage, Victor Turner has focussed on "the middle phase, liminality, when the individual is in transition between known states. This phase may be a period of marginal existence that passes, or it may become a role extended though a lifetime entirely given to the principles and practice of uncertainty, exploration, innovation, rebellion, and many varieties of nonbelonging."[9] The very experience of being marginalized, if it doesn't simply end in dehumanizing the individual or group, may be a threshold experience which allows passage away from the culture's stereotypes. "Folk wisdom has it that old people 'are the same as they have always been, only more so.' Liminality—being socially in limbo—anomie, rolelessness, neglect, and social irrelevance may have the complex advantage of leaving old people alone, to be themselves only more so."[10] There is a 'moment' of marginality in turning 65; there is an increasingly powerful experience of marginality the further one lives past 65. We need to tap into the energy in this marginalization for breaking the power of the culture's images so that new images and metaphors can prevail—images which are consistent with our religious understandings.

FACE-TO-FACE GROUPS
AS A MEANING-MAKING STRATEGY

This task is unlikely to be successfully accomplished, however, unless the people affected together form new meanings in community. There are, of course, some individuals who achieve, apparently on their own, a freedom from the constraints of the culture's images of aging. Particularly some very old people come to an "often noted but little-studied toughness, fearlessness, idiosyncrasy, and creativity [. . . from a] combination of social irrelevance and personal autonomy."[11] But there is a much greater chance that this will happen, I suggest, when there is a community of meaning which arises from people who recognize themselves to be under the same oppression.

I recognize that this emphasis on the community character of meaning runs counter to much of what we assume about individuality. There is a certain resistance, perhaps particularly Western, to self definition in terms of community of origin or belonging. Metaphors of the self-constructing individual (self-actualization, becoming, adaptation) which stress the role of the individual in expanding patterns of life seem closer to our experience. As much as we might know with our heads that the "we" exists, and exists powerfully, before the "I," it seems or feels that the "I" is far more dominant than the "we." But of course this is not so. The question is not whether or not we will be shaped by a community of meaning but rather which community of meaning will shape us. "The individual, before it can determine itself, is determined by the relations in which it is enmeshed. It is a fellow-being before it's a being."[12] New meanings and metaphors arise in community, and are learned in community. When the people affected by the culture's language about aging form new meanings in community they will overcome its oppression.

Language, like knowledge, is not interest free. The language we use about aging, particularly language which shapes action and feeling, bears within it agreements about divisions of power frozen into a particular social reality. The images and metaphors of aging which I have described are not for the benefit of the old. In fact, they are oppressive, sometimes physically and financially, by making a less-than-human standard of living acceptable for the old, and more often personally by giving the old marginal roles "that represent a limited range of stereo-types — serene, detached, disengaged, wise, and so on — all closely related to maintaining a manageable problem population, easily institutionalized and patronized."[13]

How can we create a climate in which those affected are likely to find that it 'makes sense' to struggle to new meanings in community? How can people learn how to be aged as they once had to learn to be adult? We can find some clues in the phenomenon of women's groups which were the place where women's liberation began. Betty Friedan writes:

> In the last 20 years I have journeyed from the confrontation with what I called the feminine mystique to my current confrontation with the mystique of age. I am now applying the lessons of 20 years spent articulating a new direction and redefinition of the role of women, to addressing our negative, dependent stereotypes about age. [. . .] The analogies between the two movements are not perfect, but they are illuminating.[14]

Let me draw out a few characteristics of these groups in which older adults are becoming free from the domination of the culture's metaphors and images.

1. Participants in these groups will recognize that they are indeed oppressed. Participants in these groups will recognize and name in this face-to-face community their common experience of oppression. Here the individual will move from the experience of *problems* of aging to the experience of oppression and marginalization of themselves by the culture.

2. Participants will recognize that their oppression is for the benefit of someone else. Oppression always has to do with the distribution of power. Genuine dialogue which does not just repeat the clichés of the culture is the starting point for a recognition that the culture's metaphors of aging are not for the sake of those who are growing old.

3. Participants in these groups will be peers. This does not always preclude some participation by younger people; nor does it

preclude specific, contracted professional interventions. The recognition of other older adults as peers will be difficult for most older adults who are very aware of their own individuality and who have—like us all—been socialized to despise the old. Yet peer groups are core to this proposal. It was only when women stopped looking to men for life and began to find life in the sisterhoods that they were able to liberate themselves. It is only when those who are marginalized in a certain way (by reason of age, or gender, or class, or ethnicity) form their own groups that the process of liberation can begin. Those who are defined as old by the culture's metaphors and images (or who recognize that they will inevitably so be) must form groups where their own experience of present or future social inferiority and marginalization can be named.

4. Participants will come to the insight that they will only be freed when social changes take place. A whole range of verbal and symbolic realities embody the culture's metaphors of aging. Women recognized this in exclusive language, in the media's use of young women to sell products, in unequal pay, and so on. Aging persons will have to name and counter the verbal and symbolic realities which embody the culture's metaphors of aging.

I recognize how difficult it will be to convince and engage people in the work of these groups. I am encouraged by a number of signs of hope.

RITUALS AND WORSHIP

Face-to-face groups alone will not radically alter cultural metaphors on aging. Participants must also find in their public worship clear acknowledgement that they are fully part of the community of faith. Where the sacred is named and humanity is defined in a relationship to God there is no place for excluding anyone from a claim to full humanness. But as a matter of fact, it is evident that Church and Synagogue are not much different from the culture in their marginalizing of older adults, although we may do this more by our silence than by direct action.

There is a trend in our society, fueled no doubt by commercial interests, to celebrate ritually more and more events in childhood, including graduation from kindergarten! There is no such trend in the 15 or 20 or 30 or more years after age 65. "Retirements and funerals are crude markers for the stark beginning and end of old age; in between there is a universe of differentiation that remains a cultural wasteland for each to calculate and navigate alone, without the aid of ritual, ceremony, or symbol."[15] It is clear from our cultural metaphors of aging why this is so. A favorite example of how much it is so is our silence about that most important day of the month for most older adults, the third, when Social Security checks arrive. In many Church traditions, virtually anything can be lifted up in prayer. What does it mean that this important reality is never mentioned?

Perhaps a way to begin to challenge those cultural images will be to create rites and symbols in our churches which celebrate or grieve the transitions of aging. There is every reason for a religious community, if it believes it has any wisdom about aging, to publicly ritualize retirement in a way that emphasizes what the retiring person has to offer society. Likewise ritual is important for the many positive accomplishments of aging: the creative use of leisure, the successful struggle to achieve integrity, the resistance to despair in the face of sickness or diminishments, the joy of establishing new relationships.

But we need also to devise rites for losses: "giving up the family home, transferring property and privilege to children [. . .] relinquishing one's driver's license, moving into an institution [. . .] and the many large and small events that are usually thought of as failures and signposts indicating that the end is ever nearer. [. . .] While these are undeniably negative and painful events, the clear public acknowledgment of them by others who accept and care about them has clarifying, healing consequences that redefine relationships and identities for all those involved."[16]

The purpose of these rituals, in part, is to make public what society sees as increasing marginalization in a context where there will be some incentive to struggle together to common wisdom. I acknowledge the enormous difficulty in creating rituals for Church communities which have lost skill even in celebrating rites of passage into adulthood—where there is some precedent. Nevertheless there are here, too, small signs of hope to be shared and fostered. The challenge to the Synagogue is somewhat different here, as Jews have a clear ritual for passage into adulthood and do not recognize that age ever excuses from study and practice of the law.

NEW METAPHORS FOR AGING

What new metaphors for aging will arise from the communities of faith which struggle together for new, counter-cultural images and metaphors of aging? It was not long ago that I thought I knew the answer to that when I spoke about aging as a spiritual journey and as a wisdom-quest. In one sense I still appreciate those metaphors. Negatively, they give a basis for challenge to self indulgence, for criticism of "the long years of vapidity in which a healthy elderly person does little more than eat and play bingo, or consume excessive amounts of drugs, or expect a self-indulgent stupidity to go unchecked."[17] Positively, they catch a sense of heroic and risk-filled tasks undertaken with others — marks of successful aging, where the journey is to death and the stake is the human spirit. They also leave room for aggressiveness, independence, individualism, interdependence, competitiveness, future orientation and the like — all of which are seldom praised as virtues in older adults.

My hesitation is two-fold: firstly, to assign the wisdom-quest or spiritual journey to one part of the life-cycle is in some sense to aid and abet the process of marginalization; and secondly, to choose metaphors apart from participation in community with those who are affected by our culture's metaphors is to short-circuit the very process. However, this does not deny that there is a particular piece of wisdom which can only be accomplished by those who were born near the beginning of this century and who bear the memories of the transition from early industrial society to today's highly technological society. We need their memories of other relationships to earth and social order to provide options for ourselves.

In any case, if there is success in countering the prevailing cultural metaphors about aging, new metaphors and images will have to arise — counter-cultural, humanizing metaphors which will keep the whole of human life human. It is my conviction that this is a fundamental task for Church and Synagogue as they consider religion and aging.

NOTES

1. Frank Waters, *The Man Who Killed the Deer*, 2nd ed. (Athens, Ohio: Swallow Press, 1970), p. 24.

2. Ronald Blythe, *The View in Winter*, (New York: Penguin, 1979), p. 73.

3. Thomas R. Cole, "The 'Enlightened' View of Aging: Victorian Morality in a New Key," in *What Does It Mean to Grow Old: Reflections from the Humanities*, eds. T. R. Cole and S. A. Gadow, (Durham, NC: Duke University Press, 1986), p. 122.

4. Constance Beresford-Howe, *The Book of Eve*, (Toronto: McClelland & Stewart, 1973), p. 16.

5. Erdman B. Palmore, "Retirement: Causes and Consequences," *Advances in Research* 9 (1986).

6. William May, "Care of the Aging: a Clue to the American Character," *Cross Currents* 32 (1982):193-209.

7. Peter Berger and Thomas Luckmann, *The Social Construction of Reality*, (New York: Penguin, 1966), p. 162.

8. Ibid.

9. Barbara Myerhoff, "Rites and Signs of Ripening: the Intertwining of Ritual, Time, and Growing Older," in *Age and Anthropological Theory*, eds. D. I. Kertzer and J. Keith, (Ithaca, NY: Cornell University Press, 1984), p. 310.

10. Ibid.

11. May, p. 17-22.

12. Russell Jacoby, *Social Amnesia*, (Boston: Beacon Press, 1975), p. 34.

13. Myerhoff, p. 311.

14. Betty Friedan, "The Mystique of Age," in *Productive Aging*, eds. R. N. Butler and H. P. Gleason, (New York: Springer, 1985), p. 37.

15. Myerhoff, p. 312.

16. Ibid.

17. Blythe, p. 22.

Faith Development
in the Adult Life Cycle

Kenneth Stokes, PhD

SUMMARY. The Faith Development in the Adult Life Cycle Project, completed in 1987, studied the relationship between the aging process and faith development. It is not limited to older adults, but addresses issues of faith development throughout the *entire* aging cycle.

A telephone sample of 1000+ persons was surveyed by the Gallup Organization, supplemented by in-depth interviews with 41 persons. The data were analyzed in the context of seven hypotheses related to the topic.

Among the findings were: faith development is not significantly related to age; it does not differ qualitatively by sex, although men's and women's approaches to faith development are subtly different; and there is a positive correlation between psycho-social health and faith development.

INTRODUCTION

The Faith Development in the Adult Life Cycle Project was conceived in 1979 to seek to identify and better understand relationships between the changing dynamics of faith through adulthood. What began as concern among a few leaders came ultimately to involve well over 1200 persons and 23 religious organizations in a major research endeavor.

The study was not limited to older adults, but addresses one dimension of aging — faith development — in its fullest scope from the end of adolescence to the end of life. It was predicated on the prem-

---

Kenneth Stokes can be contacted at 9709 Rich Road, Minneapolis, MN 55437.

ise that faith changes and develops throughout life much as do the physical and psychological dimensions of life.

The Project sought to bridge a gap and provide a dialogue between developmental psychology and theology. This paper reports the Process and the major Findings of the study.

The late 1970s saw a growing interest in human development within the social sciences, particularly among adults. The popularity of Sheehy's *Passages*[1] extended that interest to a much broader audience. At about the same time, the concept of *faith development* was attracting attention in religious circles. Unfortunately, however, there was — at that time, at least — little dialogue between the two disciplines.

These factors, and others related to them, led the Religious Education Association of the United States and Canada to initiate the Faith Development in the Adult Life Cycle Project in 1979, and a similar concern motivated 22 other denominations and organizations to join the REA, as Partner organizations, in sponsoring the research.

Nineteen eighty was a year of preparation, and the Project itself was conducted between 1981 and 1987. Its oversight was vested in a Steering Committee elected by the Partner organizations. The writer served as Director of the Project throughout its six years.

THE PROCESS OF THE STUDY

The Design of the Research

The Project was carried out in three phases. Three broad goals, one for each phase, were established at the outset of the study.

- *Phase I Goal:* To establish hypotheses, based on current literature and research, about the dynamic relationship, actual and potential, between the patterns or causes of change throughout the adult life cycle and the development, in terms of both growth and regression, of an individual's faith.
- *Phase II Goal:* To test the hypotheses, by means of questionnaire and/or interview methodologies, with a statistically valid sample of the American and Canadian populations.

• *Phase III Goal*: To suggest and develop the implications of the findings of the research design identified in Goals I and II for individuals and those in the helping professions related to ministry, counseling, and education.

Two principles were fundamental to the Project's philosophy throughout the study. They are:

— *Participative Research*. From the beginning, an effort was made to involve as many interested persons as possible in the Project, primarily through a major Symposium and thirteen Regional Conferences.
— *Practical Application*. This Project differs from most research studies in that it does not end with the collecting of data and reporting of findings. Rather, the research is but the beginning, with the expectation that from it will come the development of practical resources for religious professionals based on the findings.

The word "CHURCH" was and is the generic term used to describe all configurations of people gathered for worship, education, fellowship, and/or service in a religious or values oriented setting. Similarly, "MINISTRY" is used in the broadest sense of the word. Far from being limited to clergy or professional religious leadership, MINISTRY is here meant to symbolize *all* forms of people-oriented activity related to the life of the CHURCH.

Hypotheses

The research tested seven hypotheses. The Project sought to determine the extent to which these hypotheses may or *may not* be true. The findings indicated varying degrees of validity in each.

The seven hypotheses were determined primarily on the basis of input from participants in a 1981 Symposium on the topic, and served to focalize on issues of primary concern for the study. The hypotheses chosen were as follows.

1. *The dynamics of FAITH DEVELOPMENT are different for men and women.*
2. *FAITH DEVELOPMENT does not occur at a consistent rate or in a uniform way throughout adulthood, but rather in varying patterns of activity and quiescence directly related to specific chronological periods of the ADULT LIFE CYCLE.*
3. *There is a relationship between periods of transition, change, and crisis in one's life and his or her FAITH DEVELOPMENT.*
4. *FAITH DEVELOPMENT is positively related to one's involvement in organized religion.*
5. *FAITH DEVELOPMENT is positively related to one's involvement in social issues and concerns.*
6. *FAITH DEVELOPMENT involves struggle leading to both cognitive and affective change.*
7. *FAITH DEVELOPMENT is positively related to one's involvement in educational experiences.*

Preparation for Data Collection

During the first half of 1981, a Research Team reviewed the literature in several fields related to the study. Their report, *The Hypotheses Paper*, included both this background material and 21 *suggested* hypotheses which *might* be addressed by the Project. This paper provided the basis for discussion at an international Symposium held at the College of St. Thomas in Minnesota in 1981. This paper is preserved as Chapter 3 of *Faith Development in the Adult Life Cycle*.[2]

The hypotheses were refined at the Symposium. The primary purpose of the Symposium was to identify the central issues to be researched, focused through these hypotheses. Symposium leadership included Malcolm Knowles (Adult Education), James Fowler (Theology), Mary Wilcox (Moral Development), Gabriel Moran (Religious Education) and Winston Gooden (Developmental Psychology). Each presented a critique of the *Hypotheses Paper* from the perspective of his/her discipline, which was followed by a panel discussion of all five leaders and, ultimately, involvement of the entire group. Nearly 300 people from 40 states and provinces participated in this preliminary dialogue, which set the direction for the subsequent research.

Phase I was completed with the publication of *Faith Development in the Adult Life Cycle* in 1982.[3] It contains the *Hypotheses Paper*, the reaction papers presented by Knowles, Fowler, Wilcox, Moran and Gooden at the Symposium, and reflections on the Symposium topic and experience by seven persons representing different vocational perspectives.

Phase I provided the theoretical framework for the actual data collection anticipated in Phase II. By the end of 1981, a preliminary research design had been developed in cooperation with the Princeton Religion Research Center, an affiliate of the Gallup Organization. An instrument for telephone interviews in the United States and Canada was created and was pretested with a sample of 557 respondents in May and June, 1982.

The decision was made to utilize two research methodologies for gathering the data. A full telephone survey administered by the Gallup Organization was designated *Module 1*. A need was also seen for a complementary data gathering module utilizing in-depth interviews as its basic research methodology. In 1982, Dr. Connie Leean, a member of the Lutheran Church in America Research Staff, was chosen to direct this model, which was designated *Module 2*.

Gathering the Data

Module 1 involved a quantitative survey methodology conducted by the Gallup Organization, which provided the Project with a statistically valid cross sectional analysis of the population. It was complemented by Module 2, which used in-depth, qualitative interview and analysis methodology designed to probe more deeply into meanings of responses than was possible in Module 1.

A. Module 1

The Module 1 survey was part of the weekly Gallup Omnibus in March, 1985. Telephone calls were made to randomly chosen households representing a cross section of the U.S. population balanced geographically, socio-economically, racially, and by age.

Approximately 30 questions were put to 1000 + respondents. Since all answers were concise, they were easily computerized for analysis.

B. Module 2

Forty-one men and women representing a variety of geographic (Canada and U.S.), ethnic, religious, life style, and economic backgrounds were interviewed by Module 2 researchers skilled in the in-depth, qualitative method of interviewing.

Each person interviewed was asked to set out, on a form provided by the interviewer, a "tapestry" or historical overview of his or her life. On this form were noted important events in that person's life, in addition to perceptions of particular faith/values/religious attitudes at specific times. In the interview/conversation that followed, the interviewee was invited to "flesh out" perceived relationships and meanings of items on the tapestry. Dialogue between interviewer and interviewee helped focus on the significance of specific experiences for the person's faith development, and often lasted several hours.

The transcript of each interview was analyzed in two ways: a "faith-stage" coding, based on Fowler's stages of faith development,[4] and a "psycho-social" coding, based on the Eriksonian theory of psycho-social development.[5]

The gathering and preliminary interpretation of the data were completed in July, 1985. These findings provided the basic grist for further discussion and evaluation at the Regional Conferences.

Regional Conferences

Since the ultimate purpose of the Project was to involve practitioners in exploring the implications of the research findings for those involved in ministry and other helping professions, thirteen Regional Conferences were held between August, 1985 and March, 1986 throughout the United States. In May, 1986, a similar conference was held in Canada.

The Regional Conferences brought together, in relatively small units of people, professionals in education, counseling and ministry for three days: (a) to receive and evaluate the findings of the Module 1 and Module 2 data collections; (b) to explore the implications of these findings for ministry; and (c) to recommend the development of resources which would assist the practical application of the data in ministry and other helping professions.

Project Director Kenneth Stokes led the 13 U.S. conferences and participated in the Canadian conference. Other members of the research team participated in most of the conferences. There was a Theological Resource Person at each conference to provide leadership in the exploration of the theological implications of the study.

Although the review of the research data formed the focal point of the Regionals, each of the conferences went far beyond the study itself in theological discussion, network building, and that special enrichment that comes when people from different traditions interact around issues of common concerns. The evaluation forms reaffirmed, at Regional after Regional, the values that take place when Catholic, Jew, Orthodox, Protestant, and those of other faith traditions engage in meaningful dialogue together.

COMPARING THE MODULES

As was noted previously, the need for two approaches to the research was recognized from the beginning, and the topic was studied from two perspectives. Module 1 and Module 2 address a common concern — the relationship between an individual's movement through the adult life cycle and his/her faith development — but do so in very different ways.

The strength of Module 1 is its statistical validity. The Gallup Organization held telephone interviews with a random sample of the U.S. population. The Project benefitted from the highly sophisticated abilities of this research organization.

Module 1's objective questions were computer-tabulated and cross-tabulated to provide an almost limitless variety of comparisons and responses by specific subgroups and the ability to correlate answers from one question with those of others. The objectivity of the interview kept interpretative bias to a minimum. Gallup interviewers may only read the questions; they are not allowed to clarify or interpret in any way, thereby assuring as complete neutrality as possible.

The major weakness of this approach is, of course, the limitations of a simple answer survey for the complex issues involved in a person's faith attitudes. There are limitations of a telephone inquiry impacting the home situation. A "cold call" with no preparation for the depth of the questions asked may provide spontaneity, but often at the expense of time for the person interviewed to reflect upon his/her responses.

The Module 2 research methodology was designed to examine the complexities of faith and life cycle issues in greater meaning and depth, through conversational dialogue between two persons. Each interview was actually the exploration of an individual's "faith story," and was highly subjective. Although this provided a richness of content, it was often extremely difficult to structure the interview around specific questions or outlines, and to compare responses in terms of particular beliefs, issues, or concerns.

This subjectivity also let to problems in analysis. The analysis procedures for Module 1 and Module 2 were quite different. With Module 1, answers to questions were in the form of a favored response option (on a predetermined scale), while Module 2 responses were open-ended and narrative. Thus, Module 1 analysis is a direct tabulation of numerical response values, yielding mean scores, etc., which can be correlated and cross-tabulated with other scores. Module 2 responses were eventually given numerical values after a specific scoring framework was applied to them. While established criteria for making such coding judgments were used, the coder's interpretation makes this a more subjective process than the process used in Module 1. To control for subjective bias in Module 2 analysis, each transcript was read and analyzed by a minimum of four members of the Module 2 research team, and every effort was made to analyze the Module 2 data as carefully and objectively as possible.

In summary, each of the modules has its strengths and its weaknesses. As has been noted, the greatest value of the study comes from the utilization of *both* research methodologies and the comparison of their findings. Some readers find more meaning in the Module 1 objective approach, others in Module 2's greater subjectivity. Perhaps the richest rewards come in experiencing the "dialogue" between the two approaches to research.

A SUMMARY OF THE FINDINGS

This section provides a *summary* of the research findings. They are developed in more detail in the Project *Report.*[6] This section summarizes the major findings in the context of the study's hypotheses.

As has already been noted, the seven hypotheses were chosen to provide the foci for the data sought. They were determined, in large measure, by the participants in the 1981 Symposium through small group process and plenary discussion.

A hypothesis is a statement that may or may not be true. The validity of any given hypothesis was not necessarily assumed, but they provided a framework to address the basic issues of the study.

Hypothesis 1: The Dynamics of FAITH DEVELOPMENT are different for men and women.

Both modules agree that there are no *major* differences between men and women in terms of the content of their faith development. The statistical analysis in Module 1 reveals essentially the same responses by both sexes to questions regarding the amount and nature of faith change. Module 2 makes essentially the same statement. Both modules agree, however, that there are *significant differences* between men and women in the ways they *experience* faith. For example, Module 1 indicates more salience—that is, the degree to which people reflect upon and give meaning—to their faith on the part of women than of men. Module 2 indicates that women tend to remain in Faith Stage 3 (Fowler), which is characterized by socialization and dependency. However, once women have moved into the autonomy and objectivity of Faith Stage 4, they appear to have an easier time moving through it to the more complex and multi-dimensional experiences of Faith Stage 5.

Women have a greater emotional involvement in their faith development and explore more fully the meaning of the faith experience. Significantly more women than men define "faith" as "a relationship with God" while more men than women define it as "a set of beliefs." From both modules, it is apparent that women are more likely than men to turn to others in times of life crisis.

These findings illustrate an essential reaffirmation of the traditional images of masculine and feminine approaches to personal and social matters. Women tend to be more affective and appear to seek and find a fuller and richer meaning in their faith experiences than do men; men tend to be more objective and reserved in their faith expression. Women appear to be more socialized and often dependent in their faith development; men tend to be more internalized and independent in theirs. Women are more likely to talk about their faith experiences, while men tend to keep them more to themselves.

Hypothesis 2: FAITH DEVELOPMENT does not occur at a consistent rate or in a uniform way throughout adulthood, but rather in varying patterns of activity and quiescence directly related to specific chronological periods of the ADULT LIFE CYCLE.

This hypothesis stemmed from Levinson's research with males which shows a clearly defined alternation between periods of stability and periods of transition throughout the life span. Our purpose was to see if there are similar patterns of change, *related to age itself*, in people's faith development.

Little was found in either module to suggest any predictable clustering of faith change or development based on chronology throughout the life cycle, with two exceptions which will be noted below. It is apparent that faith development is highly personal in nature and is influenced much more by the social context in which a person lives than by chronology.

Two exceptions to this general finding emerge in the research. Module 2 indicated increased psycho-social tension in the period between 36 and 45 years of age. This tension is not always seen as a crisis of faith, per se, but is probably focused around struggles for meaning which often characterize the "mid-life crisis" period. Since the Module 2 research also shows a continuing positive correlation between the dealing with and resolution of psycho-social tensions and faith development, it seems apparent that mid-life — a critical time during which basic presuppositions are rethought, some discarded, and others restructured in a process of making sense of life's meaning and purpose — may well also be a crucial period for faith development, although often not recognized as such.

The other exception to the general finding is that both Module 1 and Module 2 affirm that there is an identifiable pattern of rethinking and reorienting one's faith structures in the decade of the '20s. Young adulthood is the period during which the child becomes an adult. It is a time of disengagement from one's parental home and the establishment of one's own identity in the adult community. This often includes rejection or modification of previous religious and values orientations and the acceptance, often tentatively, of one's own and sometimes very different philosophical and theological life perspectives.

Two other factors appear to be significant in the Hypothesis 2 research. First, it is apparent that the factors affecting faith development are more closely related to culture than to chronology. Today's rapid social change affecting all age groups probably is more important than a person's age in its effect on that person's faith development patterns.

The other factor is that, in both modules, most people had difficulty seeing their psycho-social development and transitions as related to their faith structures. The tradition of faith as "unchanging" makes recognition and acceptance of faith as "developmental" extremely difficult for many people. Put another way, the study indicates that although most people *do* experience faith change, most feel uncomfortable or even guilty about admitting it.

Hypothesis 3: There is a relationship between periods of transition, change, and crisis in one's life and his or her FAITH DEVELOPMENT.

The Module 1 data establish a definite correlation between major life events and changes in faith. It is not clear, however, which is the dependent and which is the independent variable. What is important, however, is that the research affirms the hypothesis: changes in faith *do* occur more during periods of transition, change and crisis than during times of relative stability.

Module 2 adds an important dimension in noting that those interviewed see faith growth more as a process of "maturing" or "evolving" than of "changing." Also, in the analysis of what impacted faith development, it is not so much the *fact* of a crisis or transition in a person's life that affects her/his faith as it is *the way* the individual deals with, learns from, and grows spiritually because of the experience.

Both modules clearly indicated that crisis may lead to either "stronger" or "weaker" faith. These terms are really ambiguous, however. A person, experiencing crisis, may well "lose faith" in terms of finding his/her traditional faith structures less than adequate while, at the same time, may actually be "growing" into new and perhaps more mature understandings of her/his faith. It is a paradox of our religious enculturalization that a faith which is maturing and developing is too often perceived as retrogressive because it involves the rethinking and perhaps rejection of traditional ideas.

Hypothesis 4: FAITH DEVELOPMENT is positively related to one's involvement in organized religion.

From the Module 1 research, all indicators affirm a high correlation between faith change and participation in organized religion. It is not clear, however, whether it is the involvement that leads to "more faith" or the faith that leads to participation. It is probably a combination of the two in which each contributes to the strengthening of the other.

Module 2 finds a similar positive correlation but, with its ability to probe more deeply into meanings, suggests that involvement in a religious community, per se, is not as much a factor in one's faith growth as the *quality* of that experience. Those who report church relationships that sponsor or encourage the spiritual quest and the exploration of meaning find that it is this active searching process in the context of the faith community, not membership or routine participation only, that makes the difference.

One interesting, if disquieting, Module 1 finding comes from the responses to question 2, in which those interviewed were asked to indicate whether they felt "a person's faith *should not* change throughout life" or "a person's faith *should* change throughout life." Although 2/3 of the total sample believe faith *should change*, church members are more likely than non-church members to indicate that "faith should *not* change." Obviously, many active participants in organized religion feel that the idea of a changing faith is not good. Interestingly, to another question (15) about questioning one's early beliefs, even among those who indicated that they did not believe faith should change, nearly 4 in 5 (79%) hold the position that faith is made stronger by questioning early beliefs. These responses provide a paradox that has intriguing implications for ministry.

In the Module 2 survey, many people report that they see themselves as more "spiritual" than "religious." Apparently, the word "religious" carries with it a connotation of the traditional establishment whereas "spiritual" suggests a more personal, direct relationship between the individual and his/her Ultimate Authority. This may be significant since both modules list responses that indicate some degrees of discomfort in the church relationship on the part of a majority of those indicating themselves as church members. For that matter, Module 2 reports a significant number of interviews which indicate that a religious institution or religious training had been a negative factor in shaping their attitudes toward religion.

Module 1, coming at the same issue from a different perspective, reports that, when asked where they would turn when faced with a problem or crisis, of a list of nine choices, "seek help from a religious counselor" was ranked *sixth* and "discuss it with a class or group in your church or synagogue" was ranked *last*. It is apparent, from these data, that relatively few respondents see the faith community as a major resource at times of difficulty or personal crisis.

Obviously, there are valid and understandable reasons for these negative findings, but they do point up a significant paradox surrounding this hypothesis: although there is a strong affirmation of the importance of the church in people's lives, there is also a high level of criticism regarding the institution. Perhaps this is but an example of human nature which indicates that we often are most critical of those persons and institutions for whom we have the most affection. If so, then, the critique can actually be seen as a form of affirmation. However, the findings related to this hypothesis suggest implications for ministry that the church must address if it is to adequately meet the needs of its people.

Hypothesis 5: FAITH DEVELOPMENT is positively related to one's involvement in social issues and concerns.

Module 2 sees a clear correlation between social involvement and faith development. This is understandable because Module 2 defines faith development in terms of Fowler's structure, which itself includes a strong component of social, ethical and global awareness as characteristic of the higher levels (4 and 5) of faith development. Put another way, since Fowler's structure sees social involvement as an indication of higher faith stages, the correlation is built in and this study affirms the findings of Fowler's research, at least in this relationship.

Module 1 is more guarded in its statement. Most of its data do not provide either a clearly positive or clearly negative correlation, but rather a mixture of responses.

This may well stem from different interpretations of Module 1 phraseology. For some, the idea of a "change in faith" leads directly to higher (Fowler) faith stages that clearly involve increased social consciousness. For others, a "change in faith" may well be a "born again" experience which motivates the individual toward a more fundamental and *personalized* religious experience in which social issues play a lesser part.

It is apparent, however, that the balance of the data suggests tentative support for the hypothesis.

Hypothesis 6: FAITH DEVELOPMENT involves struggle leading to both cognitive and affective change.

Unfortunately, this hypothesis was poorly worded. It involves two different variables in its statement — addressing the factor of "struggle" (which is difficult to define in research terms) *and* a comparison of cognitive and affective change. Although the intent of the hypothesis was to measure the degree to which "struggle" was a part of the faith development process, the data from both modules addresses this issue only partially.

Module 1 correlated responses to several questions to indicate that those who report faith change in their lives were about equally divided between those who saw it primarily as the result of thought and discussion (cognitive) (46%) and those for whom it was primarily a strong emotional experience (affective) (49%).

Another Module 1 tabulation indicates that the change came for nearly six in ten (59%) at a time when life was essentially "stable" or "normal" and for four in ten (40%) at a time when life was "turbulent" or "chaotic."

Further analysis indicates that in both these situations where faith change was viewed as primarily cognitive and those in which it was viewed as affective, the life factors "stable/normal" and "turbulent/chaotic" were approximately equally divided. Also, the greater the degree of faith change that takes place (viz. "totally different" vs. "a little different"), the more likely it is that "struggle" will be a part of it.

What is apparent from these Module 1 data is that the "cognitive" and "affective" dimensions are essentially equally divided, as are the life factors "turbulent/chaotic" (which may suggest "struggle"), and "stable/normal" (which may suggest "non-struggle") in faith change. This effectively compartmentalizes the population into four relatively equal quadrants: "cognitive"/"turbulent/chaotic," "affective"/"turbulent/chaotic," "cognitive"/"stable/normal" and "affective"/"stable/normal."

Module 2 lifts up the importance of *"balance"* between the "cognitive" and "affective" dimensions, both in terms of psychosocial health and faith development. The Module 2 research indicates that where there is significant imbalance between the two, the individual's development in faith suffers markedly.

Neither module, therefore, indicates that any given frame of mind or emotional context is *necessary* for faith change or development. Changes in faith happen at turbulent times for some, but for others a time of stability seems to be more appropriate for change.

Hypothesis 7: FAITH DEVELOPMENT is positively related to one's involvement in educational experiences.

Module 1 states that those who reported their faith has changed since age 16 are more likely to have read the Bible, to be involved in church study groups, to have studied social issues, and to have read books dealing with life's meaning than those whose faith has not changed.

There is a similar, and even greater positive correlation between these factors among those who experience positive faith change than among those for whom the changes have led to "less faith." Further, there is also a positive correlation between the amount of formal education and the reporting of a significant change of faith. The more schooling one has, apparently, the more open s/he is to faith change. However, a similar positive correlation is found between the amount of formal education and the judgment that one has "less" faith now than at age 16.

These several separate factors interrelate in an interesting way. They suggest that the experience of education apparently makes one *more open to* the development of one's faith, but this development quite often leads to a judgment of "less faith" rather than "more faith."

This again brings us to the recurring paradox, already noted in the context of Hypothesis 3, which is based on a problem of definition. It is obvious that many of the responses, particularly in Module 1, are based on a feeling that rethinking and reformulating one's faith structures, which usually leads to the rejection of traditional beliefs and symbols, is seen as "less faith" (because of the factor of rejection). In actuality, a case may well be made that although the individual may have "less" faith in terms of childhood beliefs, s/he may well have developed "more faith" in terms of the richness and new meaning of faith s/he has discovered as a mature adult.

Module 2 is much more sensitive to this concept of maturing of faith than Module 1 can be. It sees the importance of non-traditional forms of education—sharing faith stories, dealing constructively with religious differences, intercultural relationships, etc.—in stretching the mind to experience new ideas which stimulate the development of a fuller and more meaningful faith.

It is apparent that education which enriches and challenges the mind and spirit is, in fact, positively related to one's faith development. The problem, however, is that creative and challenging educational experiences for adults are, apparently too often, missing or minimal in most of today's churches. Conversely, the data (particularly Module 2) show that creative and challenging involvement of people in spiritual questioning and growth can and does have a positive impact on their faith development.

CONCLUSION

The *Module 2 Report* states an important overall finding which in many ways summarizes the study. It indicates a fundamental *positive correlation* between faith development and life cycle dynamics. It states that there is evidence of a very strong positive relationship between psycho-social health (Erikson measure) and faith development (Fowler stage theory). This comes through clearly in Module 2, is generally affirmed by Module 1, and appears to be substantiated in an overview of all the data. If this be true, then there is the affirmation that counseling and education, particularly as directed toward helping people deal with life tensions and problems, do have a direct bearing on the development and growth of people's faith.

Limitations of the Findings

In reviewing the data discovered in this study, Project leaders become profoundly aware of the complex interrelationships and undiscovered implications of the findings, so many of which necessitate further, more definitive research. We recognize that these findings are limited in scope, but see them (and hope the reader will see them) as a *beginning* of exploration into the intriguing world of the relationship between the dynamics of FAITH and those of the LIFE CYCLE.

We recognize that gaps in the research will be critiqued by scholars and practitioners, and value these comments and criticism. It is our larger hope, however, that these same gaps may well provide springboards for a wide variety of academic and professional studies that will seek to *close the gaps* by building upon and amplifying this research into a more complete and far more comprehensive body of data. Such further research can and will have an important impact on the performance of ministry and, through it, the significant touching of people's lives as they grow in faith throughout the journey of life.

Finally, we remind the reader of the far more detailed material to be found in the Project *Report,*[7] and invite further exploration of topics of particular interest among those pages.

NOTES

1. Sheehy, Gail. *Passages*. New York: E.P. Dutton & Co., Inc., 1976.
2. Stokes, Kenneth, Editor. *Faith Development in the Adult Life Cycle*. William H. Sadlier, Inc., 1982.
3. *Ibid*.
4. Fowler, James. *Stages of Faith*. New York: Harper & Row, 1981.
5. Erikson, Erik. *Childhood and Society*. New York: W.W. Norton, 1950.
6. *Report of the Faith Development in the Adult Life Cycle Project*, available from the Project Office: FD/ALC, 9709 Rich Road, Minneapolis, MN 55437.
7. *Ibid*.

Ministry with Retired Professionals

James J. Seeber, PhD

SUMMARY. Retired professionals have unique needs and skills to offer in continuing service to society. In Protestant religious thought, all persons have a life-long calling to carry out, so, while employment may change or end, use of talents and skills should be continuous. Altruistic principles may help retired professionals to rethink later life "callings." Churches and synagogues have an extraordinary challenge in assisting retired professionals to seek more than entertainment in their activities and to advocate for their meaningful participation in society.

A number of recent gerontology studies have noted that retired populations are increasingly heterogeneous. Other studies have made sharp distinctions between different aged or functional levels of retired persons. One functional set of categories deals with the "Active Elderly," "Transition Elderly" and "Frail Elderly." Another study has divided people into the "young-old," and the "old-old." One caution to exercise then is not to generalize too widely about "older people." Another caution is to disregard images of retirement, prevalent a few years ago, which picture retirement as a traumatic and devastating experience, especially for males. One recent study notes, "there appears to be no great trauma associated with retirement, however, and many men apparently find fulfillment and happiness. It may be that, in reality, retirement as an event has little to do with well being. Anecdotal evidence suggests that some men thrive and others decline after leaving work."[1]

James J. Seeber is Special Administrator for Religion and Aging Programs, Institute for Religion and Wholeness, School of Theology, 1325 N. College Ave., Claremont, CA 91711.

This paper was prepared for "Spiritual Maturity and Wholeness in the Later Years" Conference, Claremont, California, April, 1987.

185

One category of retired persons which requires special note are retired professionals. Some of the traditional functions of work (source of income, structure of life routine, source of status and identity, context for social interaction-friendships, source of meaningful experience-vocation) may be more important to the professional than to the hourly wage earner. Thus retirement may hold special problems for the professional person.

What constitutes a profession? One scholar suggests that it is characterized by high prestige, technical complexity, and extensive role expectations.[2] In general, a professional has internalized a set of principles by which a certain discipline is guided and is (or should be) capable of applying the principles to a variety of subject matters on a variety of topics. The transferability of principles is part of what distinguishes professional roles from technical roles. Only a few studies have examined the unique needs of retired professionals.

Benz[3] and Rowe[4] in two different studies found that many retired academic professionals tend to remain identified with their disciplines. Rowe reported that many attend professional meetings, read in their field and continue research. He suggests that the academic commitment to the search for knowledge is a deeply ingrained value for academic professionals.

Stokes and Maddox found that blue-collar workers reported greater retirement satisfaction than did white-collar workers, apparently the result of a higher intrinsic satisfaction with work among the white collar workers.[5] In contrast, Streib and Schneider found a higher positive attitude toward retirement among professional workers than among clerical and unskilled men and found pre-retirement attitude to be the most reliable predictor of retirement satisfaction.[6]

It is not entirely clear as to what these differences mean. However, it seems likely that professional workers might well value the professional prestige and identity and could hold a favorable view of retirement so long as they were able to retain some professional status and identity in retirement. Retired military officers and retired clergy often retain their titles (Colonel, Bishop, Rabbi, etc.) which may well reflect a strong abiding identity with the position and be a source of continuing prestige. Crowley found, looking at workers as a whole, that only health and income adequacy had a significant negative effect on the sense of well-being in retirement.[7] Overall, these studies suggest the need for more careful scrutiny of the particular needs of retiring professionals.

Several authors, following a continuity theory of life-style, have argued that the way the decision to retire is made and the pre-retirement attitude strongly affect the retirement experience. The opportunity to phase into retirement over an extended period of time, as is being done in some places, also has been supported on the same basis.

The present paper contends that the potential for actively continuing to use some of the professional skills in ways that are seen by the individual as of interest and support the values of his/her professional identity should contribute to higher retirement satisfaction. Society, in general, sanctions only two types of roles for retired persons, viz., leisure consumers and volunteerism. The continuity of professional activity, perhaps in some new way, could be a specialized volunteer role. However, in a society that is highly materialistic, practicing the modified professional role for some partial pay would enhance its meaning a great deal more.

LIFE-LONG VOCATION: A THEOLOGICAL POSITION

What is being proposed then has a clear theological referent, particularly in the Protestant understanding of vocation as the God-given call to use our talents so long as we have life and breath. The Biblical world had no concept of retirement as it has been established in modern society. However, there are clear teachings about the meaning and virtue of work and use of skills in Scripture. The Original Testament in general views honest toil as the task of persons, either as punishment for ejection from the Mythical Garden (Genesis 2) or as the natural lot of humanity. The New Testament takes a more positive view of work. The familiar Parable of the Talents (Matthew 25:14-30) teaches that skills and talents are God-given and are to be used or lost. Further, they are to be used in ways that are *of value to the Creator* from whom they come. One prominent scholar extrapolates from the parable that three benefits accrue from the positive use of such talents. First, there is fellowship with others using their God-given talents well. Numerous philosophers and social scientists have discussed and examined the tendencies of artisans and working groups to gather into professions, trade unions and associations. Second, with the good use of one's talents comes increased gifts. A parallel statement might be that there arise broader settings in which one's talents may be exercised. Third, with the increasing gifts or settings in a moral universe comes increased responsibility for the best exercise of those gifts. The judgment of the parable is clear. Failure to utilize the gifts in a creative way results in their loss.[8]

Professionals retiring from careers who consider the teaching of this parable would need to ask how their talents can continue to be used in a constructive way. To retire to a life of idleness would clearly be seen as sinful and worthy of condemnation.

In I Corinthians (12:4-11), St. Paul makes a powerful appeal for the variety of gifts people have and for the importance of their use because they are given by the Spirit of God to each person. He goes on (I Corinthians 12:12-31) to describe the mutual interdependence of persons as the community of faith (the body) which is maintained by the exercise of their God-given talents. "For just as the body is one and yet has many parts, and all of the parts of the body, many as they are, form one body, so it is with Christ" (I Corinthians 12:12). While these are spiritual gifts which are described, the importance of all gifts or talents is implied. In fact, major professions today are listed among the spiritual gifts St. Paul enumerates. He speaks of those with ability to cure the sick (medical professions), administration (ubiquitous in bureaucratic modern life), and ability to explain things (education professions). Throughout St. Paul's teaching, talents (of whatever kind) are gifts given and work is to be done not merely for personal gain or to please men, but in order to glorify God (Ephesians 6:7-8; I Corinthians 10:31).

Finally, it should be noted that the New Testament holds a positive value of secular work. Christ was a carpenter and St. Paul continued as a tentmaker during most of his missionary journeys. The early church was made of people who followed a variety of careers and were encouraged to praise God in all that they did. Part of St. Paul's salutation to the Thessalonians says, "To this end we always pray for you too, asking our God to find you worthy of the call he has given you, and by his power to fulfill every desire you may have for goodness, and every effort of your faith, so that the name of our Lord Jesus may be glorified in you and you in him" (II Thessalonians 1:11-12). The Thessalonians were called to be a community of faith, but they were also called in their several occupations to glorify God through their work.

Through the centuries, the church came to understand a *vocation*, a God-given calling, as exclusively for church careers. A two-level society of those in sacred orders and those in secular work was established. One of reformer Martin Luther's strongest teachings was that every Christian has a calling from God to follow. He pointed out that persons in nearly every station or rank of life can serve God and that all service ranks the same with God. "This means that a servant, maid, son, daughter, man, woman, lord, subject, or whoever else may belong to a station ordained by God, as long as he fills his station, is as beautiful and glorious in the sight of God as a bride adorned for her marriage or as the image of a saint decorated for a high festival."[9]

Most modern theological thought works to debunk the divisions between sacred and secular that have existed since the Renaissance. Gone is the separate realm of supernatural versus natural. Gone is much of the separateness of the kingdom of grace (the church) versus the kingdom of law (the world) in Luther's terms. Gone is the understanding of a sacred calling to one's life work as the exclusive domain of church workers. Donald Heiges summarizes modern Lutheran's understanding of Everyman's (and we infer Everywoman's) vocation:

> Everyman's vocation outside the household of faith involves the perennial task of glorifying God in every facet of life. Vocation summons Everyman to glorify God through loving service to all persons; it challenges Everyman to make the most fruitful use of the gifts God has given; and it equips Everyman by divine command and grace to be effectively instrumental to God in the realization of his purposes for the whole creation."[10]

Elton Trueblood, the encyclopedic Quaker philosopher, likewise suggests that vocation should be understood as applying not only to persons entering religious occupations, but to other persons as well. "If ours is God's world, any true work for the improvement of man's life is a sacred task."[11] Trueblood describes the *principle of vocation* in terms of several qualities which are especially applicable to the retiring professional considering how his/her skills can continue to be used. These include:

1. substituting a concern for working where there is a true human need that can be served rather than more personal advancement;
2. seeking a place and activity that may offer effectiveness in service over mere security;
3. seeking a chance to be creative in the use of one's professional skills;
4. possibly providing public service of undoubted integrity free of charge to those who need it most;
5. and last, ideally, to create work that lasts, that has merit sufficient to have lasting qualities.[12]

The principle of vocation as a life-long calling means that one may retire from a profession or job or a series of jobs, but continue to seek ways of exercising the God-given talents he/she has to serve God through serving others. Such an understanding offers a sharp focus for the potential transition of retiring professionals. Ideally, it might introduce a four-step process of change:

1. person is employed full-time, building economic credits and resources toward retirement life
2. reduction of full-time work to part-time allowing time for reflection, counseling, and career-transition planning
3. retirement from previous employment; training or shifting of professional skills to some new part-time "vocation"
4. perhaps gradually increase the time for retirement activities or personal care as needed while continuing in some "service role" using one's skills occasionally

What is proposed here is radical in two ways. One, it rejects the idea of discontinuing the use of skills one may have spent a professional career developing. Two, it presumes that we have a task, a *vocation* (calling) to actively serve others through the use of our talents all through the so-called retirement years. Unfortunately, many older people have accepted societal images which devalue the elderly by encouraging them to be what Maggie Kuhn has referred to as "wrinkled babies." The Biblical-historical tradition of our Judeo-Christian tradition knows no such image of aging. The institutionalizing of retirement in modern industrial societies should not lead older persons to minimize their talents or opportunities to serve.

WHAT CAN CHURCH/SYNAGOGUE DO?

The identity of retiring professionals is bound up in the retirement roles of the society. Because of this, ministry with retiring professionals must deal with systemic change in order to broaden the options within which the theological principle of vocation can be understood and pursued. Religious institutions over time do affect the expectations of people and can help to create new role images for the later years of life. Presently the older adult ministry of most congregations provides entertainment for the active elderly and a modest support ministry for the frail elderly — usually shut-ins and residents of institutions.

A major opportunity is available for congregations and judicatories to sanction an image of vocational change, a re-tooling and changing gears, perhaps a model of gradual retirement, through an occupational winding-down. Teaching the principle of vocation as the right and responsibility of each person to seek meaningful use of his/her professional skills and helping to find or create opportunities for persons to do so may be of much value to older professionals. Preaching and counseling with middle-aged and younger persons to look toward the later years as a time to be seriously creative with their skills has exciting merit in it.

Recent political changes are supportive of softening the enforced retirement pattern. The (1979) Age Discrimination in Employment Act forbids compulsory retirement before age 70, and recent revisions forbid it at any age in certain occupational fields. Social security now encourages continuing employment past age 62 and even past 65 by increasing benefits for each month of additional work. At the same time, social security has been steadily increasing the so-called earnings limitation after persons start drawing benefits. One author notes that a whole new area of late-life career counseling is needed to help older persons consider their options.[13] In addition, the principle of vocation raises issues of changing jobs and changing professional career goals to more religious and/or humanitarian tasks for which careful guidance will be helpful. Religious institutions could help to facilitate such changes.

Another aspect of ministry could be assisting retiring professionals to be aware of and to make use of valuable programs that assist persons to use their skills. There are federal programs such as Senior Corps of Retired Executives (SCORE), Retired Senior Volunteer Program (RSVP), Foster-Grandparents (F-GP), Volunteers in Service to America (VISTA), the Peace Corps, PHENIX Programs at many universities, etc. Some denominations have begun to develop Senior Ministries. Two examples are the Seniors Education Venture through the Episcopal School of the Laity, and the "Gift of a Lifetime" volunteer program of the Presbyterian Church, U.S.A. directed by Dr. Tom Robb. The latter uses older volunteers to develop local church programs for older people. One way in which local congregations can be of help to retiring professionals who are "free lance" persons is to offer office work space. For a minimum of cost two or three or more persons can share an office and related accoutrements. In studying the patterns of continuing professional activity among retired university faculty, Lane found that lack of physical facilities had a distinct negative effect on the tendency of professionally-oriented persons to remain active in their fields.[14]

In addition to offering shared office space at a modest cost in underused facilities, congregations can encourage informal colloquia, dialogues, etc. A variety of support services can perform a major ministry with retiring professionals. It is possible to help alleviate the sense of boredom experienced by some retired persons and to ward off the feelings of uselessness which many older people dread.

NOTES

1. Joan E. Crowley, "Longitudinal Effects of Retirement on Men's Psychological and Physical Well-Being," *Retirement Among American Men*, ed. by H. S. Parnes et al. (Lexington, KY: D.C. Heath and Co., 1985): 170.

2. William C. Lane, "Faculty Retirement at a Land Grant University: A Study of Retired Faculty from Kansas State University," (Unpublished Ph.D. dissertation, Kansas State University, 1980): 182-183.

3. M. Benz, "A Study of the Faculty and Administrative Staff Who Have Retired from New York University, 1945-1956," *Journal of Educational Sociology*, 32:282-293, 1958 cited by Eugene A. Friedmann and Harold L. Orbach, "Adjustment to Retirement," chapter 30 in *The Life Cycle and Its Common Vicissitudes, Pt. 3*, pp. 634-635.

4. "The Retirement of Academic Scientists," A. R. Rowe, *Journal of Gerontology*, 27: 113-118, (1972) Cited by Eugene A. Friedmann and Harold L. Orbach, see above, pp. 634-635.

5. "Some Social Factors on Retirement Adaptation," R. G. Stokes and G.L. Maddox, Jr., *Journal of Gerontology*, 22: 329-333, 1967 cited by Eugene A. Friedmann and Harold L. Orbach, see above, p. 632.

6. *Retirement in American Society: Impact and Process*, G.F. Streib and C. J. Schneider (S.J.); (Ithaca, NY: Cornell University Press, 1971) cited by Eugene A. Riedmann and Harold L. Orback, see above, p. 632.

7. Crowley, "Some Social Factors," p. 170.

8. "Exposition of Matthew," George A. Buttrick, *Interpreter's Bible*, vol. 7, 561.

9. Donald R. Heiges, *The Christian's Calling*, (Philadelphia: Fortress Press, 1984), 55.

10. Ibid., 76-77.

11. Elton Trueblood, *The Common Ventures of Life*, (New York: Harper & Brothers, 1949), 85.

12. Ibid., 89-101.

13. "New Work Roles for Older Adults," A. D. Entine, *Generations*, vol. 4, #1, 21.

14. Lane, "Faculty Retirement at a Land Grant University," 189-190.

Reflections After the Conference

A true crisis exists in the field of religion and aging. Almost no thorough or extensive research is being done to better understand how spiritual resources and religious life contribute to successful aging nor how it interacts with other variables in later life.

Why is this dilemma occurring? Public funds are nearly impossible to receive for any sort of religion-based research effort. Recent announcement of NIA's FY'88 research grants totaling hundreds of millions of dollars contained nary a dime for study of the one practice older people continue throughout their later years, viz., spiritual habits. This dearth of support is presumed to be due to restrictive views of church-state separations. Indication of this lack of research funding is seen in that only three of the twenty-four papers presented at the Claremont conference were directly research-based. At the same time, denominations are not yet persuaded that ministry with older people needs major research or program investment.

The American Society on Aging in 1988 has acted to create a Forum on Religion and Aging which is dedicated to sharing concepts and best practice models with practitioners in both secular and religious arenas. A number of scholars and practitioners are seeking research funds to improve the knowledge base of spirituality among the aging. Cooperation between groups of scholars in order to en-

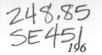
hance our knowledge using the limited resources which can be located is gravely needed. To the stimulation of that end, these papers are dedicated.

James J. Seeber, PhD